SILENCE*broken*

SILENCE *broken*

MOVING FROM A LOSS OF INNOCENCE TO A WORLD OF HEALING AND LOVE

Sara O'Meara
&
Yvonne Fedderson

*INSPIRATIONAL STORIES OF CHILDHELP USA'S
JOURNEY IN THE TREATMENT AND PREVENTION
OF CHILD ABUSE AND NEGLECT*

JODERE
GROUP *SAN DIEGO, CALIFORNIA*

JODERE
GROUP

Jodere Group, Inc.
P.O. Box 910147
San Diego, CA 92191-0147
(800) 569-1002
www.jodere.com

Book design by Jenn Ramsey
Editorial supervision and additional writing by Chad Edwards

Photography Acknowledgment
We would like to thank, along with the list below, our family,
friends, staff, and colleagues, who, over the years, have been so
gracious as to help us document our journey through picture taking.
Even though the images have been placed in *our* minds forever, you have
allowed us to share the joy of our mission with so many. Blessings!

Loren Anderson Photography • Bill Dougherty Photography
Imageworks Photography • Portraits by Merrett • Lee Salem Photography
Visual Concepts Photography • Craig Wells Photography

Childhelp USA®, Childhelp USA National Child Abuse Hotline®,
National Day of Hope®, and 1-800-4-A-CHILD®
are registered trademarks.

CIP data available from the Library of Congress

ISBN 1-58872-065-9
06 05 04 03   5 4 3 2
Second printing, December 2003
Printed in the United States of America

endorsements

For over 44 years, the humanitarian efforts of Sara O'Meara
and Yvonne Fedderson have led the way in awareness
and treatment against child abuse. *Silence Broken* is
an engrossing journey of help and healing, told by children
and adult survivors whom you will certainly come to admire,
love, and respect. It is my hope that all of us can commit
to make a difference as much as Childhelp USA.

—DAVE PELZER
Author of *A Child Called "It"* and *The Privilege of Youth*

It warms my heart to read of the dedication, support,
and love given to children in times of great need by
Childhelp USA. I truly commend the work being done
on behalf of children all over the world.

—FORMER FIRST LADY BARBARA BUSH

Great stories talk heart-to-heart and soul-to-soul.
This book overflows with heart and soul talks
that will expand your love and move you to
compassionate right action, right now.

—MARK VICTOR HANSEN
Author of *Chicken Soup for the Soul* and *The One Minute Millionaire*

Silence Broken *is a love story about two exceptional human*
beings and the children they touched, loved, and saved.
Sara O'Meara and Yvonne Fedderson take us into a world
of maltreated children, and the miracles they accomplished
that help restore our faith in the human spirit. A must read
for all who care about what is happening to our children.

—VINCENT J. FONTANA, M.D., F.A.A.P.
Medical Director
New York Foundling Hospital
Author of *Somewhere a Child Is Crying* and *Save the Family, Save the Child*

I read this book from cover to cover in one sitting.
It is so touching. The stories of these children
and the women who brought their lives to what
they should be are amazing. Sara and Yvonne,
we all love you, and always will.

—MERV GRIFFIN
Entertainer and Entrepreneur

dedication

$\mathcal{W}$e dedicate this book to the following people who have shared their love, and extended their hands and hearts to help countless dreams and miracles come true for the mission of Childhelp USA, and who have committed continued support to even more profound and fascinating projects yet to come.

To Sara's parents, Dr. and Mrs. Claude Buckner; husband Bob Sigholtz, and children Sylvia and John Hopkins, Taryn and Karl Gosch; and to her most precious grandchildren Ashleigh and John Charles Hopkins and Sara Catherine Gosch.

To Yvonne's mother, Mrs. Fred Lime; deceased husband Don Fedderson; and daughter Dionne Fedderson Archer.

To the National Board of Directors, many of whom have been by our sides since the founding of the organization: Nancy Brown, Vita Cortese, Patti Edwards, Jim Hebets, Marilyn McDaniel, Phil Odeen, Connie Olsen, Gloria Sutherland, Linda Willey, Armstrong Williams, Earl Worsham, and Don Zimmer.

To those who have supported us through their belief in our dreams, and through their dedication, financial gifts and gifts of time. To all of these wonderful hearts, we humbly thank you with unending gratitude.

contents

I am here
With a twisted life
I am here
With a twin 500 miles away
I am a boy
With a lot to handle
I am growing quickly
Becoming stronger
I will overcome this stress
I have the help of people who care
And the people who care
Encourage me and make me happy
I will one day be a father
I will do better than I knew as a child
One day I will become
A secret agent
Or maybe work for the police
I will prevent bad things from happening
I will protect all citizens
I will make it

*Written by a 10-year-old boy
from the Village of Childhelp West*

Yvonne, Cheryl Ladd, Brian Russell, and Sara.

foreword

You are about to embark on a journey launched by two women, Sara O'Meara and Yvonne Fedderson, two young Hollywood actresses, whose chance encounters—one with 11 homeless orphans abroad and one with Nancy Reagan—have led to a lifelong commitment to helping children in need. It is a story that also tells of the birth of an organization they created to address child abuse in America, which came to be known as Childhelp USA—one of the oldest and largest nonprofit organizations addressing this issue.

Silence Broken is a collection of stories told through the eyes and voices of the children who have been helped and through the everyday interaction of people who struggle to help them out of their man-made hell. Some sad, some happy, all of them touching. It has been the mission of Sara and Yvonne that the children who are brought to them, most of whom have seen the worst that life has to offer, be provided with the best atmosphere and support—as well as the best therapeutic care so they can begin to heal.

It is my hope that as you take this heart-warming journey, you realize that the intention of this book is to make us all more aware of the reality of these particular children growing up in our society today. It is a fact that each day in America, three children die as a result of child abuse in the home and more than 7,300 cases of abuse a day are reported. And at least three times that amount go unreported everyday. That's every *single* day. Whether this book helps you reach out to support a child in need or opens the door for you to come to terms with something in your own past, I have no doubt you will finish the last page with a sense of hope about what can be and is being done about this ever-growing problem.

The awareness I have obtained about this issue has changed my life, and it will change yours.

The problem of child abuse in our country first came to my attention in 1978. Shocked by what I read, I conducted a little investigation of my own and was appalled at what was and was not being reported in the press. I was so moved that when ABC wanted to do some movies of the week with me— *Charlie's Angels* was a pretty big hit on ABC at the time—I told them: "Yes. Not only would I like to do a movie of the week, but I want to do a movie of the week about child abuse."

ABC went into shock about the whole idea. "That's not what we had in mind."

"I understand," I continued, "but I'm really passionate about this, and I think somebody needs to be telling the child abuse story. It's an epidemic now in our country and nobody seems to be talking about it."

The network executives squirmed, and there was this long silence.

"Not only that," I added, "but I want to play the child abuser because that will make people understand that abuse can be happening right next door with someone you would never suspect. The public will not expect me to play a role like that. It will cause them to take notice."

At first, the executives said, "No, we don't want to do that." But after a lot of talking, and meetings, and more meetings, they saw that I was not going to change my mind. We finally made "When She Was Bad."

It was well received and shocked a lot of people. Then I went out to promote the movie on the talk show circuit. Even though we knew it was going to be a hard sell, we wanted to get people interested in the whole subject. At the time, child abuse was one of the best-kept secrets in the country.

At the end of a guest appearance on the *Dinah Shore Show*, I said, "If there's any organization out there trying to fight child abuse, please get hold of me. Call the show, and tell me who you are because I do not want to just make this movie and then drop the ball. I want to be actively involved in fighting for abused children from now on."

No sooner had I said that and walked off the set when the phone rang. It was Sara O'Meara. "Please come and see what we're doing," she said. "We want you; we need you. This is what we are about. Will you come and see us?"

"Of course," I said.

Sara explained that they already had a residential children's center in Beaumont, California. She told me that they were about to dedicate a new gate at the Village and invited me to the event.

"We'll talk afterward," Sara said. "And we'll show you what we're doing. We'll give you a tour of the facilities."

That's how it came about, and I've been with Childhelp USA ever since. I've been one of their Celebrity Ambassadors and a million other things—whatever they ask. But in order to really understand the problem and what's at stake, I think you've got to see the children and get to know them.

Most of the children who come to Childhelp have been

so badly battered and bashed; it's hard to believe the horrors they've had to endure.

On one visit to the Village of Childhelp West in Beaumont, California, I went with my husband, Brian Russell. We were bringing a trailer filled with bicycles, toys, and clothes for Christmas. During our visit, we went into one of the cottages where the children live because we like to interface with them and talk to the people who work with the children. We like to let them know how much they're appreciated, because theirs is a really tough job. They have to work against incredible odds, and it's easy for them to get burned out.

We walked into one of the eight homes, which housed two to four-year-old girls. As we came through the door, one of these little girls saw my husband and started screaming at the top of her lungs and ran away.

Brian felt terrible.

One of the social workers said, "Maybe you should stand outside for a few minutes. Her father has abused her since she was an infant. She starts screaming when she sees any man come toward her."

Brian went outside. I went to the little girl and picked her up. She clung to me—trembling and shaking. Once Brian was out of sight, she calmed down and rubbed my face with both hands and said, "This my nice mommy . . . my nice mommy."

And she wouldn't let me go.

Outside, my husband could hear the child and was horrified to think that a little girl would simply see a man and feel absolute terror. Ever since that day, Brian and I have been working side-by-side for Childhelp USA. In that one moment, that one little abused child won his heart.

This is just one of the thousands of stories that touched our hearts.

One of the reasons the problem of abused children has affected me so much is that I knew and counted on the love of my parents—how wonderfully they treated me, how valuable I felt growing up—to help me make my dreams come true. They helped me make a productive life and have healthy relationships. I now know what a gift that was. I look at so many other children and realize they've never had that gift. Worse yet not only has unconditional love been absent from their lives, but too often, they've been victims of vicious abuse. And more and more, we're coming to understand what a curse it is not only in this country but also throughout the world.

I want to honor my parents who gave me such love and support and give thanks for the grace of God. Child abuse is a problem for *all* mankind—a huge obstacle if you will—and I want to be a part of the solution—in whatever small way I can. That's why I'm so committed to Childhelp USA and support the wonderful healing and love they provide for many, many children.

Thank you, Sara and Yvonne, for allowing me to be a part of this.

Blessings,

Cheryl Ladd

Childhelp USA Celebrity Ambassador

acknowledgments

We would like to acknowledge and thank those who have played significant roles in making this book possible:

Nick Bunick
Chris and Mark Donnelly
Chad Edwards
Arielle Ford
Brian Hilliard
Debbie Luican
David Ulich

Yvonne and Sara, Hollywood Starlets on tour in Japan (1959).

introduction

After witnessing his parents murder his sister, a little boy became totally silent. No one could get him to speak. He was placed in 15 different foster homes before being sent to a Childhelp Village. No matter how hard they tried, none of the staff was able to get the little boy to speak. Finally, the man in charge of the Village's animal therapy program took the little boy to the barn and told him that Chocolate, the pony, was now his responsibility. He would have to feed and care for him. Each day after that, the little boy ran to the barn to see after Chocolate. On the fifth day, the little boy put his arms around the pony and said, "I love you" out loud. The silence had been broken, and the boy's journey toward healing had begun.

This story is but one from our lifetime of work with children who have suffered from isolation, despair, neglect, and abandonment: A story that serves to recognize that when the silence is broken, healing can begin. Stories similar to this have kept us going since the late 1950s when we first encountered the silent horror of what some children were experiencing on the "world stage." Until then, we had just been two young girls who started out our lives living in the 1950s world of *The Adventures of Ozzie and Harriet*—literally. As the actress girlfriends of David and Ricky Nelson on the hit TV show stereotyping the perfect American family, we could have never realized in the beginning of this adventure how we would come to serve children around the world. It was our first encounter with the 11 abandoned orphans we discovered on the streets of Japan that launched our mission to speak out about the tragic situations of these children—to break the silence—and find ways to bring them into an environment that would provide nurturing and healing. Sometimes, the silence can seem so loud that you must pay attention and give it a voice. It has been a labor of love and commitment that has involved long unending hours and hard work spanning decades. It is a commitment that has become a passionate pursuit—and one that has been heart-warming, gratifying, and always God-inspired.

Because we have taken action to expose the plight of these children and provide some solutions, child abuse has begun to come out from under the dark cloak in which it had been hidden for eons. Today, we know that each day in the United States alone, at least three children die as a result of child abuse. We know that most of the children who die are younger than six years of age. More children, ages four and younger, die from abuse and neglect than any other single cause of injury deaths for infants and young children.

Over 40 years and many miracles later, we are proud to say that Childhelp USA, the organization we created, is one of the oldest and largest nonprofit organizations in America dealing with child abuse and neglect. Since its inception, we have worked to make Childhelp USA and Childhelp Villages models for standards of care for abused and neglected children around the world. We have come to understand that by building a place of trust and understanding supported by an atmosphere of faith and emotional stability, these children are given a chance to begin to rebuild a sense of self-worth and create a better life for themselves.

We do everything within our power to help each child heal and reach his or her God-given potential. We want every child to realize he or she has a unique contribution to make to this world. We believe unconditional love is the foundation upon which all healing begins. And we believe that these children, who have seen the worst that life has to offer, deserve the best that we can provide. We have been shown that once their silence is broken and they start to reveal the "secret" they have been conditioned to conceal, these children can then begin to move from a loss of innocence into a world of healing and love.

This book, told through the sometimes subtle voices heard in the children's stories, through some of our wonderful staff, volunteers, and supporters, jointly with us, truly tells many of the stories that represent this incredible journey from tragedy to triumph of which we've been so blessed to be a part. The resiliency of these children is a lesson for us all. Our mission for these hurting children began over 40 years ago and continues to expand rapidly wherever God leads. Our only choice is to "show up for duty" and be open to His direction.

In Love and Light,

Sara and Yvonne

They came when they
could to be with the children.

Sara and Yvonne with children
found abandoned in the streets of Japan (1959).

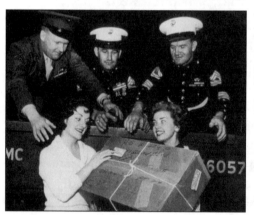

Our wonderful servicemen rush to support.

Mama Kin.

CHAPTER ONE

the beginning

SARA AND YVONNE'S AWAKENING

Yvonne and I were warm and safe in our hotel room in Tokyo, Japan after four days of a severe typhoon—one of the worst the city had ever seen. We had never experienced such fierce storms in our lives. For a couple of those nights, we had sat in our hotel room in total darkness with the high winds pounding at our windows—all power had gone out. We had all been under strict orders not to leave the hotel, and we were more than glad to comply. It was considered a "red flag" alert. No one in the city was to go outside because of the high level of destruction that had also produced dangerous and unsanitary conditions.

But at the first sign of clearing and coupled with feeling tired of being stuck in our room for days, we decided to bundle up against the cold and venture out to explore the storm's aftermath. Our youthful curiosity had gotten the best of us and fueled our sense of adventure. As we walked through the lobby of the hotel, the desk clerk asked if he could help us.

"Oh, no! We are just going out for a walk," Yvonne replied.

"But, ladies, there is a red flag alert! You're not supposed to leave," he protested, coming out from behind the desk.

"Oh, we'll be fine. We're just going out for a short walk and getting some fresh air," I shot back as we quickly exited.

Up and down the streets we wandered, amazed at the devastation before our eyes. Trash and debris scattered everywhere; people were cleaning up whatever they could salvage. Some were loading baskets with what we guessed might be food. In some places where we stepped, the mud mixed with who-knows-what came oozing up over the tops of our shoes. At times, the stench almost took our breath away. After about a mile's walk, we turned down a small side street deciding it might be wise to start back. This initial little adventure for the two of us had already been quite an eye-opener.

Suddenly, we came upon a group of small children huddled in a circle under a fallen awning in an attempt to fend off the freezing winds. The look on their faces at the sight of these two white women coming toward them expressed a silent plea for help. They were shivering; some barefooted, most with tears streaming down their faces. As we moved closer, we noticed their knuckles were cracked and bleeding from the cold, their light cotton clothing torn, tattered, and soaked through. We counted 11 of them, ranging in age from what seemed to be about two to 12-years-old.

Horrified by the sight, our motherly instincts instantly flooded us as we unbuttoned our coats and beckoned for them to come inside to get warm. Without hesitation, the children dove under one-by-one, our coats ballooning as they squeezed in. Feeling the shivering cluster against us, Yvonne and I stood there in silence for a moment looking into each other's eyes. We didn't know what to do to comfort them and pulled out our English to Japanese dictionary in a desperate effort to translate, "Where are your parents?"

Having no luck, all we could think of saying to them was, "No papa sans? No mama sans?" The children just shook their heads and cried harder.

We knew, right at that moment, what we had to do. Without speaking, we turned and slowly began shuffling our bundles the mile back toward our hotel. As we maneuvered our cargo back through the streets, we kept trying to figure out what we were going to do. What a sight we were as we maneuvered along through the mud and debris-filled streets. We had no idea whether these children had been lost or abandoned during the typhoon. All we knew was they needed a hot meal, a warm bath and a chance for their clothes to dry, and a good night's sleep—and that's exactly what we were going to give them. We were sure that when we got back to the hotel, we could find where they belonged. At the moment, there was no time for any thoughts other than to keep moving. We were all soaked through by now and cold to the bone. But we had started this trek, and there was no turning back.

When we arrived at the hotel, we stopped outside for a moment to uncover the children. Yvonne and I agreed that we would just walk them in with us right through the lobby—hopefully dodging any resistance—and take them up to our room. We put our fingers to our lips in an attempt to signal them to be quiet. With a couple of the children in our arms and the others clinging to our coats, we entered.

To this day, I distinctly remember the rush I felt going through my body as we just walked straight through the lobby with frozen smiles on our faces in hopes no one would say anything—or notice. It amazes me how naïve we were as we led this disheveled parade, smiling and nodding at the hotel staff and other guests. After all, we were actresses, weren't we? We hoped we could carry this off. (Years later, we would laugh as we shared what each other was thinking at that moment.)

In my mind's voice, I kept repeating, *Children? What children? Just keep moving, Sara.*

Yvonne said she just kept thinking, *I hope no one stops us,* and *I hope we don't see the colonel.*

Lucky for us, we didn't see him, or our mission would have stopped right there immediately. After all, we weren't even to have been out of the hotel with the red flag alert still in effect.

When we made it up to the floor of our room, Yvonne and I stopped for a moment to take a breath before heading down the long hallway.

"We made it," I said to her with a nervous giggle.

As we proceeded down the corridor to our room, the maids on the floor just looked at us curiously, wondering what it was we were doing. We closed the door behind us. With the children still clutching on to us, we looked at each other and simultaneously said, "Now what?" What we had done really hit us in that moment. We had become so caught up in our impulse to help these children that we obviously had thought through nothing more than getting to this point; we just did the next thing that seemed natural.

We began to undress and bathe the children—two and three at a time in the tub until all were clean and wrapped in whatever we could find for makeshift clothing. By the time we were through, our room looked like a laundry with clothing to dry hanging everywhere. Then we called room service and ordered up food for all. We were surprised when the order came with exactly enough plates, glasses, and utensils for 13 people. We hadn't asked for those in an effort to keep our visitors a secret. Needless to say, by that time, the whole hotel was abuzz about the two women and 11 children. So much for going unnoticed.

We decided it was time to approach the colonel about what to do with the precious cargo in our room. We realized we needed some direction and how to find out where the children belonged. Surely, we thought, they were only misplaced by the frenzy of the typhoon, and all had homes somewhere. There certainly must be parents looking for these darling children. We persuaded the maids to look after the children as we set off to find the colonel.

When we found him and began unfolding the story, his reaction wasn't what we'd expected. He hit the ceiling and informed us that this was one of the worst things we could have done. He was horrified that we had brought the children into the hotel, much less to *our* room. He explained our actions could bring about major problems for all of us because we knew nothing about these children—who they belonged to or where they were from.

We half-heartedly apologized for not thinking more before we had brought the children with us, but we refused to abandon them back into the streets. We asked whether it was true that he also had children. We remembered he had spoken about them. Would he want them abandoned if something happened to him?

We just kept at him until he finally caved in and said, "Okay, okay."

He informed us that the best thing we could do was to get them dressed and take them to one of the orphanages in the city. He would quickly compile a list for us. We were to go get the children and be back downstairs in a half hour. There was a certain tension in his order that we didn't comprehend at the time.

With a speed that would have made anyone dizzy, we gathered the children and were back downstairs where the colonel ushered us out to a waiting taxi van he had obtained with an English-speaking Japanese man. The colonel and driver agreed that the driver would act as our interpreter in our attempt to find a safe haven for these children. After a brief conversation with the colonel, he handed us the list of orphanages, and were off on our search.

By this time it was mid-afternoon, and we had little daylight left for our pursuit. As we moved down our list, orphanage by orphanage, we were told time and again that because of the typhoon, so many Japanese children had been orphaned; thus, the orphanages were at capacity. When the sun began to fade, we wondered what were we to do. We still had several orphanages on our list. We were steadfast to this commitment and agreed that we could not leave the children out in the night.

"Back to the hotel," we instructed our driver.

That time, we stopped along the way and purchased some food to take with us so we wouldn't have to call room service. We also made an agreement with our driver to meet us at a designated place near the hotel early the next morning.

Yvonne and I decided that to avoid being caught by the colonel, we would take the children up the back fire escape then to our room for the night. On our return, we had the driver drop us off in the back of the hotel. We *knew* we were asking for big trouble if we were caught. As we climbed the fire escape, I felt the adrenaline rush through my head. The two young maids on duty began giggling as they watched us pass the children through the window into the hallway of our floor. This was the funniest scenario they had ever seen. To ensure that our "stowaways" were not revealed to anyone and to get some extra blankets for the night, we tipped them with cashmere sweaters we had brought along from home.

As the morning light streamed across the city, we exited the fire escape and set out on our search once again. Hour after hour, our troop rambled through the streets in our taxi with no success. The story was always identical—no room. It was early afternoon as we approached one of the last orphanages on the list. We drove up and stopped at the entrance. While we ushered the children out of the taxi toward the door, they started pulling back and crying in unison. Although confused by their reaction, we proceeded to knock on the door. The children began speaking in gasping clips through their tears, pointing at the door.

When the door opened, we were greeted by a gentle looking man with a surprised look on his face at the very sight right before him. After a brief exchange with our taxi driver, our driver-translator informed us that the children had been living in this very orphanage before they were sent into the streets as a result of the typhoon's destruction.

"How could this be?" we asked. "Then why were they turned away?" we also asked.

It was at this point that the truth of these children's plight was made clear to us. Our driver explained that the orphanage could no longer keep these children because they are half-American and half-Japanese. The disaster had created a situation wherein so many full-blooded Japanese had been left homeless and parentless, and the Japanese government would only subsidize them—not any children who are of mixed blood.

As we stood there listening, we couldn't believe what we were being told. The head of the orphanage went on to explain that he had actually taken these children in before even though he wasn't authorized. After the typhoon, he had been instructed to take in the full-blooded children only and send these 11 children out. He apologized with a face that looked somewhat embarrassed, yet he said there was nothing he could do. He wished us luck in finding a place, turned, and closed the door.

Stunned and speechless, Yvonne and I stood in the street frozen for a moment. We had difficulty comprehending what we had just been told. So this was the reason they were abandoned—because they are half-American. Prior to this, we had just been two young girls living in what was the America of the late 1950s who knew something about the rising voice surrounding discrimination but had never witnessed it personally. The issue stared us directly in the face. We had never understood the possible complications for children born of parents of different races. These children—who were fast becoming *our* children—had become "throw-aways." They had no value—not even to the parents from whom they were born. We were enraged! This gave us the courage to go back and face the colonel.

We had no thoughts of the possible implications that these half-American, half-Japanese children would have on our lives. We had no way of knowing at that time what breaking the silence of these children's plight was going to mean to our lives. Our innocence was beginning to have cracks running all through it.

When we returned to the hotel, we explained to the colonel all we had been through and adamantly told him we were not going to walk away from the children. He took a deep breath, shook his head, and then gave us the name of a doctor—a half-American, half-Japanese man who had been running the Tokyo Gospel Missions—and in the past had taken such children into his establishments. The colonel then confessed to us that he had known that the half-American children were a problem. We hit on an issue that both governments refused to deal with at the time. It was growing to be a "hot topic."

Fueled with a newfound energy, we immediately contacted the doctor. Sadly, we found that he was leaving for the United States. But he directed us to a Japanese woman known as "Mama Kin," who he felt might be able to help because she had already taken other mixed-blooded children into her home. Once again, we loaded the children back into the van and struck out to find Mama Kin.

We were very encouraged until we arrived at her thread-bare, one-room hut with no front door in the doorway. Even the windows were without windowpanes. She wanted to help but pointed to the ten other orphans for whom she was already caring—whose looks, oddly enough, resembled the children we had in tow. Her roof was leaking; two small hibachis were fired up—one for cooking and the other for warmth. She was just serving the last of her food. She explained that she had no money to take care of her ten, much less to take in 11 more. She showed us that she only had two jackets that the children took turns wearing outside and to school.

Through our driver-translator, we learned that Mama Kin's children had also been turned away by their families in shame, and had been living, unwanted, on the streets. She had turned this little dirt-floor shack into a refuge for them. Even though her place was meager, we could readily see that she was filled with love and light. We told her if she would help us with our children, she could trust that we would also find help for the other children. We could look into her eyes and see she was someone *we* could trust. Finally, she agreed to keep our children, and we promised to return the next day. (Later we discovered that her name meant *golden one* in the Japanese language. She proved to be every bit that—and then some.)

Yvonne and I decided that the only place we could ask for help was from the servicemen attending our show that evening. We weren't sure what might happen when we broke the silence about these half-American children we had found wandering the streets. Yet we were sure that some of their fathers, if not the majority, were quite possibly the result of some of the servicemen on R and R (rest and relaxation) from Korea where they were stationed. We were there to entertain and didn't know whether they would take offense if we brought this up, causing us to be in trouble. But that chance we had to take. We had made a promise to Mama Kin—and the children.

As we went through the show that night, Yvonne and I could hardly concentrate on our performance. When it was over, instead of leaving after our applause, we just stayed center stage. Our hearts pounded; I don't remember who started talking first. But by the time we were done, we had spoken out about these children.

"Some of these might be your children, for all you know," we said. "Please, won't you help these innocent little Amer-Asian orphans?"

We then passed the hat as we pleaded with them to meet us at our hotel the next morning and come help us make the children's home warm and more comfortable.

The response was fantastic. Somehow—and some-where—we had clearly hit a nerve. The next morning, more than a dozen soldiers arrived at our hotel in an army truck filled with blankets, sea-rations, and lumber to help upgrade the makeshift orphanage—most of them young men. We spent the entire day at Mama Kin's. Some of the servicemen put in a front door, window panes, and did general repairs to the hut, while others accompanied us to an open-air market to buy more bedding, tatami mats, warm clothes, food, and other things those desperate children needed.

We discovered that these kind men were more than willing to help. In fact, they even came back on different occasions while we were in Japan. Some came back to help again, while some just came to play with the children when they could. Sometimes as I watched them interact with the children, I wondered if one of them might be part of their own story. But it didn't matter; the ones who came clearly cared. For the rest of the scheduled tour, whenever we weren't entertaining the troops, we continued to help the homeless Amer-Asian children and the kind-faced woman who had dedicated her life to housing them.

As word got out, more Amer-Asian children were left on the doorstep of Mama Kin's hut with notes pinned on them that read, "For the Orphanage of Mixed Blood." Mama Kin's home came to be our first orphanage, eventually housing more than 100 children after the various expansions and renovations that we were able to pull out of thin air with God's help.

As our particular goodwill tour was coming to an end, we went to the persons-in-charge and asked, "Is there a way that we could extend our trip and do other shows?"

They were thrilled because they wouldn't have to send for other actresses to come and do the shows. They paid us a per diem. Although it wasn't much, it allowed us to remain in Japan an additional two months and continue to stabilize the orphanage. Doing our shows at night gave us the opportunity to go to Mama Kin's during the day to work with her and the children. We continued to have the servicemen pass the hat and obtain whatever help we could beg or borrow.

Our adventures in Japan were filled with red tape and stumbling blocks. Who knows what would have happened without the kind financial support we received from our families in the States and those servicemen. Most Americans weren't as supportive at the time: The reality of just how many children had been fathered by some of our soldiers over there did not come to full light until some years later when we dealt with the same issue in Vietnam. Yet we were determined to stay with this project even after we returned to the U.S.

One of our biggest obstacles was the red tape we contin-uously faced, which set into motion major trials in our laborious efforts to manage what we were giving *birth* to. It was difficult for anyone to imagine that our efforts would amount to anything. After all, we were only a couple of young actresses. To this day, we still run up against walls. Little did we know back in those first days in Japan that this journey would be such a challenge. Yet the driving force behind our mission is that we have always known we are not alone. Even though there have been obstacles and people who have stood in our way throughout, we knew that we have dedicated this mission to God. As such, we will always have Him by our side, along with some very special "earthly angels." For that, we are truly grateful and owe our success.

The truth is we don't think much about whether we can do something. When we got this first "call" from God, we answered—no questions asked. We've never really stopped to look at the big picture. We've never bought into the fear and resistance we met along the way. We've just kept putting one foot in front of the other toward our next goal with a lot of faith, prayer, and trust. We have seemed to go from obstacle to miracle, over and over. We then came to realize that somehow, the miracle will always show up on the other side of the obstacle—if we just hang in there long enough and keep the faith. We've tackled roadblocks as if they were to be expected. We have simply remembered at all times that we are not in charge, God is. We started to break the silence of child abuse in Japan, and we're not about to let it go silent again.

We consider our work with the children in Japan to be a perfectly natural beginning as the events have continued to unfold over the years. Even though the work there was enor-mous, we, along with our wonderful volunteers, managed to build and maintain four orphanages exclusively through private funding. Together with others who cared, Yvonne and I were also able to launch a nonprofit organization and create chapters around the United States to help expand the visibility of our mission. We called it "International Orphans, Inc." (I.O.I.). This organization eventually became Childhelp USA as we brought our efforts homeward. We know that this is what God wants us to do. Someone has to give these children a voice. And it's our privilege to continue to do it.

thank you,
and i love you

A LETTER FROM JAPAN

Dear Mama San Sara, and Mama San Yvonne,

I write this letter to you to give you feeling of thanks from all of us. We all gathered around in circle speaking about how we have clothes. We can go outside to walk to school warm for you have given us jackets and shoes. Our tummies are full and Mama Kin watches over us. At night we have our own tatami mats and in our prayers we always thank God you picked us up off the streets.

We remember that day very well by each moment for we were so frightened and cold. When you came to us, you sure looked different. You had pretty faces and your hands were warm when you gave us a hug. It felt so good when we got under your very big coats. We did not know why you stopped to see us because you did not even look like us. We never had been in a hotel before and that was exciting, but very scary. We wondered where we would be taken next?

When you smiled, our hearts talked back to us. They

said, "These are our mama sans for this time." That made us feel good.

When you left us at a broken down house without a front door, you promised to come back—and you did. The lady, Mama Kin, you left us with was nice to us too. She had other children like us. When morning came and we saw you come up to the door, we all smiled, jumping up and down. Some of us screamed, which was not nice, but we were so happy to see your faces.

You brought kind men in uniforms of America to help make our broken down home not be broken anymore. I remember a pair of red socks you put on my feet. It was the first time they were not cold in a long time. All of us here have talked and we have thought maybe you are the angels with skin on that people talk about when they speak of God's helpers on earth. You did not let us go, or forget about us.

You continue in our lives and send money, big, big boxes full of wonderful things we need—and even pictures. We could not believe that people we didn't even know in America sent money to take care of us. It changed our lives forever. You let us know you love us. Without you, where would we be? Nowhere—we would be no more. Now we have thanks in our hearts and breath for you. Now we have other boys and girls added to our family, which gets big now.

We had never been on a subway train before we came to say goodbye to you at the airport when you came to visit. We were happy to surprise you when Mama Kin taught us the music "God Bless America" in English, and we all sang it for you right there in the airport. It sounded like very funny words to us, but we saw it made you smile and have tears in your eyes. You cried and laughed, and cried and laughed. Mama Kin said it was because it touched your hearts. Some of us had tears too. We were sad to see you go, but knew you would be back. You always keep your word and come back.

We want you to know we love to touch your hearts, and so we are all saying together—we love you! You saved us for a new life with Mama Kin. We won't forget you ever, Mama Sans Sara and Yvonne. Never! Ever!!

Thank you, and I love you,

Akiko

Sara and Yvonne entertaining the children (1959).

Yvonne, Sara, and Mama Kin at the first orphanage (1964).

Mama Kin receiving the "Woman of the World" award.

The men loved being with the children.

Each and every child was so precious to us.

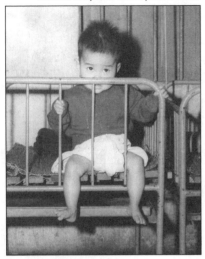

A smile to warm the heart.

We couldn't believe these beautiful children
had been abandoned.

A birthday party at the orphanage.

hello, vietnam!

THE STORY OF OPERATION BABYLIFT

It's interesting how we spend so much of our time planning out our lives, only to have them take a sharp turn in another direction. At least that seems to be the case for Sara and me.

We had spent seven years working with our four orphanages in Japan. It was 1966, and there was a controversial war raging in Vietnam. It was a time of great questioning in this country. Many of our living standards and principles were being challenged abroad as well as on the home front. We were quickly being propelled out of the idealism of the 1950s into a period that was all about breaking the silence through "love-ins" and loud protesting. It was a time of burning bras, burning draft cards, and ingesting lots of drugs—families were being torn apart. Sara and I were not sure we understood the eruption going on around us. We knew our eyes had been opened wide to a different world by what had happened in Japan, and we could see some of that similar pain in the eyes of the youth of America at that time.

We were surprised when we got a call from our local congressman, James C. Corman.

"I want you to know that I've been watching your efforts in Japan," the congressman told us. "And I've delivered many documented reports about the two ladies who've helped so many Japanese-American children. I know all about the organization you set up. I've told Congress about your dedication, and how almost 99 percent of your funding goes to helping the hundreds of Amer-Asian children in Japan, and how you two started your work out of Sara's garage. We want to honor you for what you have done."

"Us?" we asked. "Are you sure?"

"Very sure," the congressman replied.

Since we never dreamed that our actions would have warranted congressional recognition, we were filled with excitement as we discussed what we would wear to the event. As we sat in the plane en route to Washington, we were overwhelmed by the fact that we were about to stand in front of Congress and be honored.

"Why do you suppose the commandant of the Marine Corps is going to be there?" Sara wondered.

I pondered the question a moment. "I really don't know. But remember that over the years, the Marines and the Navy have helped us ship children's clothing and toys to Japan for our orphanages. Maybe they just want to thank us on behalf of the men."

Suddenly, Sara turned and asked, "What about that Marine-based program called the 'Civil Action Program,' where people in communities get involved in sending clothing and supplies to Vietnam? You know, gifts at Christmas, medical supplies, that sort of thing. Do you suppose they want us to do the same thing that we've been doing in Japan for the orphans in Vietnam?"

"Maybe," I responded, "but we can't possibly take on another thing."

"Absolutely not," Sara agreed. "We'll have to decline."

There was no way we could take on anything in Vietnam. We had now started our own families and saw no way to add anything else to our already busy lives.

Not wanting to appear ungrateful, we decided to draft a speech, just in case. We spent the rest of the flight between Los Angeles and Washington, D.C. writing an emphatic but gracious refusal speech, carefully weighing each word. It was along the lines of: "Thank you so much for putting your trust in us. But as you can see, we have already taken on almost more than we can handle." When we finished the speech, we felt much better. If we were going to say "no," we could at least feel secure that we'd be doing it with grace.

Being recognized by Congress was a great honor complemented with several eloquent speeches and awards. Afterward, General Wallace M. Green, the commandant of the Marine Corps stood up.

"You women have done such a wonderful job in Japan with International Orphans," he announced. "And now, we'd like to request that you do the same thing with the half-American, half-Vietnamese orphans in Vietnam who need help, too. They're being discriminated against in a war-torn country. These children are literally dying on the streets."

We exchanged secret glances as blown-up photographs of Vietnamese children were projected onto a large screen. He showed us pictures of closed-off areas behind barbed wire where sick, starving children stared at the camera through huge dark eyes, sitting in beds that looked like cages. Some had lost limbs from the land mines, while others' faces were almost unbearable to view.

Our hearts began to sink to our stomachs. We glanced at each other as the tears welled up in our eyes, and we stood staring at those beautiful children's faces. I am sure we were both thinking, "Oh, God. How could this be happening?"

"As you can see, the need is tremendous," Gen. Green

continued. "Very few people are doing anything to help solve this problem, so we hope you will."

We had no trouble visualizing the horror that these children were experiencing. The pictures were vivid and our hearts started racing up into our throats. Could it be that the problem we uncovered in Japan was more widespread than anyone realized? Were these children to live as the "throw-aways" also? We looked at each other, and in that silence, knew we were both feeling the same thing. God had spoken to our hearts once again. We were presented with another opportunity to do what we realized in that moment we were meant to do.

"We'd love to!" We sang out in unison—we didn't even have to think about it.

We had no choice, and evidently, we were both in total agreement. So much for gracious refusal speeches. It took five hours on the flight over to figure out how we were going to say "no" and less than a minute to say "yes." It was clearly time for another leap of faith.

While we boarded the plane for our trip home, we couldn't believe what we'd done. We hardly spoke a word the whole way home, thunderstruck by the impact of what had just occurred. We could hardly keep up with our Japanese orphanages. Yet we had committed ourselves—and our volunteers—to doing even more. Not only would we have to present this new challenge to our board but how would we ever raise the money? It seemed that our original efforts toward breaking the silence of these abandoned half-American children was about to take on an even larger voice: Hello, Vietnam!

We agreed that soliciting even more volunteers to help with additional fundraising was the answer. When we got home—after receiving the "go ahead"—we kicked into high gear, stepping up our fund raising and coordination of the efforts of this greatly expanded group. We branched out by creating a broader base of chapters outside of the International Orphans, Inc. of Los Angeles that included Santa Barbara; Bel Air; Buenaventura; Riverside; San Diego; Fresno; San Francisco; Orange County; the Inland Empire; and Palm Springs, California.

Our work in Vietnam fast became a huge success because of the help of so many of our *earthly angels* and the wonderful troops—along with the Marine Corps Reserve Officers Association and the Navy League—who were our unsung heroes. With their assistance, we managed to build five orphanages in Vietnam, which included Protestant, Catholic, and Buddhist sites. Then, one day, several members of the Seabees, a branch of the Navy, phoned us from Vietnam to report that wounded children in the Vietcong bombings were being left to die on devastated battlefields.

We were deeply touched by the fact that our servicemen, young men and women no more that 22 or 23 years old, were so worried about these children. They told us they could pick up the healthy ones and take them to the orphanages, but where would they take the wounded children? Nurses were at a shortage, and over there, children couldn't be admitted to a hospital unless someone signed for them and stayed by their side, administering to their particular needs.

These uniformed men showed us the true heart of the American serviceman, moved and haunted, searching for a solution to an intolerable problem. How could we say "no" when they began pleading with us to do something, offering to give up a percentage of their meager salaries toward building a hospital?

Our work had quickly escalated since the beginning. But at this point, it was taking an even larger leap. Aside from the regular fundraising, we had the additional need for medical equipment, medicines, and vitamins. We had no idea how we would ever pull it off. But once again, with God's help, we managed to find the necessary supplies we needed. Lieutenant General Lewis W. Walt, a three-star general, served as our Vietnam liaison. He arranged for us to ship supplies over to where they were needed. In fact, it was the general himself who opened that hospital for us, the first of its kind to support the half-American, half-Vietnamese children. Eventually, the hospital and our orphanages would care for all children, regardless of whether they were of mixed race.

Lt. Gen. Walt kept us abreast of the progress by frequent phone conversations and sent us photographs from the various building sites each step of the way. We loved to receive them, especially when we saw the finished products. But our real rewards came when, at last, we received pictures of the children with smiling faces. As ceaseless as the work was for us to meet all of our needs for the Japanese and Vietnamese sites, photographs of happy children who were clothed and fed and healing kept us going. The lieutenant general even came to Los Angeles to appear at several of our fundraisers.

Those years, from 1966 to 1975, all merge together in our minds. Chaplains, nuns, and missionaries on the other side of the world taught the children about God and prayer. We were also able to build a school because these children had neither an education nor any means to get one. Our journey continued to be paved with many obstacles like the monsoons that came yearly, yet we were also blessed with miracle upon miracle that kept us inspired to go on. We had given our word to Congress that we would keep going, but more importantly, we had given our word to God. Therefore, we never considered stopping or giving up hope.

Once, Lt. Gen. Walt called when one of the orphanages was bombed.

"No children were lost," he assured us.

"Thank God."

"Yes," he agreed. "But the bombing greatly damaged the roof, and it will have to be repaired immediately; you know that monsoon season is close, so we have less than a month. If we don't repair it quickly, a lot of children won't have a roof over their heads when those storms hit."

We had no funds for this!

All of our donated money was already designated for specific projects, and *robbing Peter to pay Paul* was out of the question. We were under the gun; we needed to raise about $17,000 in 30 days. That may not sound like much money today. But in the late 1960s and early 1970s, it was a great deal—more than we knew how to find.

On the eve of the deadline to begin the repairs, we had done everything we could think of, spoken to everyone we knew, and had only raised half the money. All of our options were exhausted and the lieutenant general would be calling that night to see if we could give him the go ahead. Needless to say, we were extremely upset; we wanted to tell him to start the construction but couldn't do that with only half the money needed raised.

Sara dropped me off at my house that evening, and feeling dejected, headed home to receive the call that was coming within the hour. It was a dark night—the moon was nowhere in sight; it had been a cloudy day so there were no visible stars. Our mood was as dark as the sky. As Sara approached the post office, she looked at her watch to check the time. Was there time, she thought, to stop in to pick up the mail and make it home for the call?

Sara dragged herself out of the car, went inside, opened the post office box, and began thumbing through the mail.

Among the usual array of letters, she was surprised to see an envelope with "Disneyland" written in the left-hand corner. That was curious; we had never had a relationship with Disney up to that point.

When she opened the letter, she couldn't believe what was inside. There was a check, made out to International Orphans, Inc. for exactly $17,000.00! "This is for your Vietnam project," the letter read. "It's from our Disneyland Wishing Well, and we want you to use it for your children in any way that you see fit."

They had no idea we needed funding for the roofs, much less this exact amount.

Once again, a miracle!

Sara drove home teary-eyed and extremely grateful, ran into the house, and called me.

"Yvonne, you won't believe it. There's a check from Disneyland for exactly the amount we need!"

We were both in tears. God had taken care of us once again. That's the way our life works. Often, it's down to the wire, but something always comes through. We must forever do our part, but God is the *Maker of Miracles*. We've never yet had to turn down a real emergency request.

Every time we've said, "Yes, we'll do it," God has provided. It's a test of faith to hang in there, not knowing until the last moment. And God *knows* we've had lots of those "last moments" along the way. But each time when we're right on the edge, it always works out. Reminding each other of this serves as a great boost to our faith, and the stronger our belief, the more we feel willing to take on.

In late 1974, Lt. Gen. Walt was in town to appear at one of our fundraisers when he asked to speak with us privately.

"Ladies," he said over coffee, "I have something to tell you—something that very few people know. But I think it's important for you to hear this now. In a very short time, I expect to receive orders from the president to pull our troops out of Vietnam. It'll happen at a moment's notice, and when the order comes, we'll be out within days."

With jaws dropped and mouths open, we could not believe what we were hearing.

We were just about to speak when the lieutenant general stopped us and sternly asserted, "Sara and Yvonne, listen to me. I don't want you to send over any more money at this point because we don't want it to fall into the wrong hands. And when I get the call, I'm telling you right now: I don't want to hear a word about the children. There's absolutely nothing I can do. Do you understand? It's going to be hard enough to evacuate our men, so I don't want any problems concerning the children. I've got enough to deal with. Okay?"

Lt. Gen. Walt acted tough, but we knew he was really a big, gruff teddy bear who loved the children as much as we did. It all seemed too far-fetched that we would leave Vietnam at the height of the war. And we couldn't bear the thought of abandoning the half-American children. We just listened and nodded. We all had seen the upfront and close images of the war via TV and the terrible things that were happening over there. But why would we retreat? America had never pulled out of a war before. It felt so unrealistic to us, and that was the last we heard until about four weeks later. By that time, we had chosen just to forget we ever heard anything. That was not going to happen.

Then it came.

"Sara and Yvonne," the lieutenant general was at the other end of the telephone.

We happened to be together, having one of our endless meetings.

"Hi," we said smiling. We were always happy to hear from him.

"Are you both there?"

"We are," we replied in unison, each on an extension phone.

"Remember what we spoke about the last time we were together?" he asked.

Sara and I looked at each other. Suddenly we felt a deep hollow in the pit of our stomachs.

"Yes," we answered, our voices quivering.

"Well, ladies, this is it. We're evacuating. I'm working night and day to get this accomplished and . . ."

"But what about the children?"

We knew that if these children were left behind, they would be killed simply by virtue of being half-American. It would be the focus of the North Vietnam soldiers taking over to do away with anything that—or anyone who—was connected to America. The orphanages would be a first target since they knew Americans were funding them. The children would be part of that target of elimination.

"Now, don't you start on me," he said. "I already told you this was going to happen, and there's nothing I can do. I'm so sorry, but that's the way it is."

We looked at each other in shock, tears filling our eyes.

"But we have to get our children out of there," was all we could think to say.

We didn't know what to do, but we had to think of something. If we didn't, we believed the Vietcong would line up the abandoned mixed-blooded children and shoot them. Hadn't we seen them doing that so many times on TV? It was too terrible to imagine. We didn't sleep at all that night, alternating between calling one another and sobbing.

Finally, I said to Sara, "Listen, Congress asked us to set this whole thing up. Now, do they really expect us to leave these children there and just abandon them? We can't allow that to happen. Maybe it's time for us to go to Congress and ask *them* for help. We can't remain silent on this."

"That's right," Sara agreed, struggling to speak. "Let's call Congressman Corman immediately and appeal to him for help."

When we reached him, he assured us that he would help us in any way he could.

"We need airplanes," we both said. "We need to have those children evacuated. We'll work around the clock and do whatever we have to, but we simply *cannot* leave them there."

The congressman sighed, "I'll see what I can do and get back to you right away. I feel your anguish, and I am with you on this."

To this day, we don't really know how he did it. But we got a call from him within 24 hours.

"If you can organize the children, I'll get the planes. You process the children. We'll pick them up in 'Nam, and fly them stateside. You understand you'll have to meet them and figure out what to do with them when they arrive. You'll need to organize the entire operation from your end."

"No problem," we said—having no idea what we were going to do.

From that point on, we stopped counting miracles. The whole experience was one tremendous miracle; we had no time to count anything but children. For the next three weeks, the lights were never off in our homes or offices. As soon as word was out that our troops were coming home, people began calling us about the fate of the children. The caring people who had contributed money to our cause wanted to know what we were doing about the children and how they could help. It was the most wonderful feeling to have count-less people reach out and be concerned for our orphans.

Volunteers showed up from who-knows-where, and each person scouted out his or her own little area outside our building. We literally ran out of inside space. There they sat, lists of children in one hand, a telephone in the other. We were all running on nervous energy. At one point, a volunteer reached into the large box of donuts donated by a local bakery, only to discover none were left. Sara and I had unconsciously polished them all off in our nervousness. We still laugh about that, but laughter was at a premium otherwise. Our only joy came from watching how people were willing to show up in a time of crisis. It validated our faith in humanity.

For weeks, we got almost no sleep. Decisions had to be made, logistics had to be coordinated with the service that was providing the planes, and adoption agencies had to be enlisted. Since our organization wasn't an adoption agency, it was crucial that we lined up with several of them once we had processed the children. We needed to find prospective adoptive parents from all over the world who could be approved and processed to assure that homes would be ready upon the children's arrival.

The media were constantly photographing us throughout these emotional weeks. Somebody showed us a newspaper article describing what we were doing as "Operation Babylift." So that became the identifying name of our quest. Everyday there was a new set of problems that needed immediate solutions. One day, a reporter asked me what he could do to help. That was when we were looking for people to process and care for the children at the airports. We already had our supply of volunteers for the office. I looked up from my desk in a haze.

"We need people whom we can clear to meet the babies at the airports and stay with them until the adoptive parents show up. Please print that for us, and tell them where to call."

The response to the newspaper articles asking for volunteers kept our spirits going. Many people offered to be there, to open their homes, to give us pretty much whatever we needed. Since there were far too many children and planes to all arrive at the same place, we coordinated planes to land in San Francisco and Seattle, in addition to Long Beach. Some were even to fly into Canada. Admiral Richard Bird, bless his heart, turned the entire Long Beach Naval Base and his men over to us—and our mission.

Arrangements quickly fell into place. Pallets were laid down on the floor of the Long Beach Naval Base gymnasium, anticipating the arrival of the babies. Each baby would be wearing a numbered bracelet or name tag on his or her clothing with at least a first name (some did have last names), and an individual volunteer would be assigned to a child. The trickiest part was that until we got word that a particular plane had taken off, no one knew either when it would be landing or at which location. That meant calling volunteers at a moment's notice to advise them of when and where to meet the children.

"We'll need special access to the airport," one of the volunteers reminded us. "How will you know us?"

We thought for a second. "Tie a yellow ribbon around your antenna. Then the Navy officers will know to let you through."

Everything was moving forward. The time for the airlift to begin was near, and we were about to accept our first planeload of children—well over 250 orphans. When we received the telephone communication that the plane had taken off, everyone cheered. It felt like NASA—cheering a shuttle takeoff. We were exhausted and ecstatic, but there was no champagne popping—just an enormous wave of hugs and tears of relief. We still had most of our work in front of us; we had to make certain that the volunteers were informed of the time and place to meet the plane, but the evacuation was beginning—at last.

Before we made the first phone call to set the next phase in motion, we received horrible news. The first plane had not made it out after takeoff. In the horror of such a massive evacuation, there had been an explosion that had brought the plane down in a rice field not far from the airport. Suddenly, someone called from the other room for us to come to the TV. Then, they flashed a shot of our crashed plane. Most of the crew were killed, along with many of the children. The injured survivors were picked up. Some were brought to our I.O.I children's hospital there, while others were taken back to the orphanage and immediately reprocessed for the next available plane.

All we could do was sob—we were devastated. After all our efforts, we couldn't believe we had lost so many children and crew with the first flight. But we had to keep moving, swallow our sorrow, and carry on—something like being in a battle. We stopped for a moment of prayer, and then began to focus on the children yet to come. There was no time to lose. We're still not sure how we got through that one. But when the call came that the next plane was taking off, all we could think of was, "God, please get them out." Today, Sara and I still have difficulty remembering that day. All the success we have had over the years will forever be marred by the loss of that plane and so many children. I think anyone alive during that time will never forget the stories and pictures coming out of Vietnam and the effect that war had on many, many lives.

The next morning, we drove to the airport together to oversee the arrival of the first plane coming into Long Beach after that horrible crash. We felt like we were doing it all by the seat of our pants, hoping we had everything covered. We were uncertain as to whether there would be enough volunteers to receive the children, yet we simply knew we'd deal with whatever happened. But we hoped and prayed that it would all go smoothly . . . and quickly. Time meant everything; it was truly a matter of life and death.

When we turned to enter the airport, we were overwhelmed. There were hundreds of cars—as far as you could see—sporting yellow ribbons on their antennas. They were lined up, waiting patiently and waving at each other. Many were our faithful volunteers from our chapters. Others just heard the news and wanted to help. Some had no knowledge of International Orphans, Inc. at all. The news of the first plane's crash had spread everywhere, and these people were simply there to help us process a child and deliver him or her to safety. They were there for the children. For the second time in less than 24 hours, we cried our eyes out. This time in gratitude.

Finally, our first plane arrived. We all cheered and hugged each other. It was all very highly emotional from start to finish. As the plane landed and pulled up to the hangar, we all lined up and edged toward the plane in anticipation of receiving our precious cargo. The sound of the engines was thunderous. When the aircraft came to a stop, the rear doors began opening, revealing a sight we couldn't believe. A sea of children was staring out at us in wide-eyed fear. Each volunteer was instructed to board the aircraft through the rear door, take a child, and exit through the front door carrying each child off the plane to waiting cars and buses, and finally to the gymnasium we were using. Sara and I were the first to board and exit with a child in our arms.

When we first saw the cardboard boxes on the plane, we thought some of the children were dead. We then realized that the seats had been removed and replaced with these boxes to accommodate the babies, making it possible to bring out more children. Granted that it wasn't the safest way to fly. But considering the alternative, it was far better than leaving any of these children in Vietnam. Some of the children were crying and terrified, some were half-smiling, and many showed no emotion at all. They were too frightened, and many were ill. It was a sight to behold.

This went on for nearly three weeks. We can still remember the last plane landing, filled with babies in cardboard boxes, and the doctor from our Vietnam hospital. He had come back to escort the last of the children, and we were so happy to see him. As the last child was carried off in his box, we asked the doctor an important question.

"Do you know if we got all the children out of the Sacred Heart Orphanage?"

Sacred Heart had cared for literally thousands of children. The doctor took hold of our hands and shook his head.

"As we took off, we flew over China Beach. I personally saw the remaining children being lined up and shot. The Vietcong had already arrived. I saw it with my own eyes."

We felt the tears well up in our eyes. There was nothing more to be said. The babies we had gotten on the planes were saved. We realized at that moment how narrow our timeline had been and how precious our cargo really was to have made it out.

Much later, Vietnam President Nguyen Cao Ky flew over to be present at the opening of our first Childhelp Village in Beaumont, California. He came in part because he knew what we had done in Vietnam and saw what we were doing on our own soil. He wanted to express his thanks in person. He told us that almost 100,000 babies and children were saved by Operation Babylift, our orphanages, and through other efforts we had helped to initiate surrounding that time. Of course, we felt good about that, yet it was hard to come to terms with the ones we couldn't bring out. The idea of children being shot in cold blood was almost more than we could bear.

We have tremendous admiration for our servicemen who not only fought valiantly for our country but also gave of themselves to help protect the children in need. Anyone old enough to remember that time of the Vietnam War has memory of some loss. Ours will always be the loss of all of the children who didn't make it out.

To this day, remembering brings tears to our eyes. That era marked some loss of innocence for many of us, whether overseas or on the home front. It was a time when many broke the silence, and it was a time followed by great healing in this country.

On a happier note, we both are proud that one of those precious children who came out of Vietnam during Operation Babylift would go on to become the first female graduate of West Point. Amazing!

the story of loan

COMING FULL CIRCLE

When the aircraft slammed down onto the earth, the two wings broke away as it skidded about 1,000 feet through a rice paddy. It hit an embankment and bounced up, thrust forward for about half a mile, came down between rice fields, and broke into several pieces. Burning fuel and wreckage covered the ground, which was peppered with bodies. Those capable frantically began trying to maneuver through the black smoke that engulfed the scene to look for anyone alive. The sludge of the rice fields made that task almost impossible.

It had only been about 15 minutes after takeoff when the first planeload of children in what was to become known as "Operation Babylift" exploded. In early April 1975, the C-5A transport plane out of Vietnam was about 40 miles away from the Tan Son Nhut Air Base in Saigon when, 23,000 feet in the air, an explosion blew off the rear doors of the giant aircraft. The C-5A carried more than 300 children and accompanying adults—crewmembers, nurses, and volunteers. With flight controls crippled coupled with the sudden rush of decompression, the plane began to fill with smoke quickly as a whirlwind of wreckage flew in all directions. The U.S. Air Force pilots managed to turn the plane back toward the Saigon Airport and crash-land two miles short of the airstrip in what would later be recognized as a "remarkable demonstration of flying skill."

The fate of the C-5A was called "one of the worst aircraft disasters in history." Almost everyone in the bottom of the transport—the majority of who were children two years and younger—were killed. Many of the 170 or so survivors were injured. I myself was bruised and burned badly. Later, many people in the United States would view this disaster as another in a long series of tragic events surrounding the ill-fated war and ultimate evacuation that took place in Vietnam. The authorities never determined whether the explosion was a result of sabotage.

Fast forward 28 years to California, U.S.A.

I am one of the survivors of that fatal crash. My name is Tran Thi Kim Loan, and I was just over three years old when that evacuation crash happened. Because I was not an infant, I was placed with the older children in the upper levels of the aircraft. This ultimately saved my life. Many of the babies, two and younger, had been positioned in the bottom cargo compartment because there was room to stretch large canvasses—hammock style—to lie the babies side-by-side in order to strap them down for safety. Many of them were placed by twos and threes in cardboard boxes; they didn't stand a chance.

I was born in a small fishing village north of Saigon called "Quang Tri" to a Vietnamese mother and an African-American father who was a U.S. soldier. As the time approached for the U.S. military to evacuate South Vietnam, my father was taken away from our area, leaving my mother and me alone. Neither of us would ever see him again. In those last days of the war and after having been left alone and shunned by the villagers for having a "half-Vietnamese" child, my mother moved us in for a brief time with a friend who had two children of her own. And when I was only around eight months old, my mother took me to the Sacred Heart Orphanage, which was operated and funded by International Orphans, Inc. (I.O.I.). She decided that she would be unable to care for me; therefore, the orphanage would be the best chance for my survival. I would never see her again either.

I remained in the care of the staff at the orphanage until the signs that the imminent fall of South Vietnam was just around the corner. It was then that several organizations, spearheaded by Sara and Yvonne and International Orphans, Inc., banded together with U.S. military and civilian supporters to orchestrate an evacuation and adoption of the orphaned children in their care. This was the birth of "Operation Babylift." Many of the children had already been processed and cleared for adoption. There were also many in this effort, like myself, who were not yet adopted but who were cleared and fortunate enough to be a part of this massive airlift out of Vietnam. Many half-Vietnamese children were left behind. Those who weren't killed would ultimately become known as the people of the hills or the "Hill People." They weren't welcome in the cities and villages.

I have been told there was much excitement and hope resting in that first departure out of Saigon. Needless to say, the horror of the crash brought about shock and anxiousness around any flights that were to follow. But the rescue efforts did continue with rapid succession. There was only a limited window of time and military backing to pull the evacuation off. They had to keep going. They did not have the luxury of extra time for grieving. Shortly, all planes remaining would be used to remove soldiers, any ambassadors and politicians, embassy staff, foreign correspondents, and their families. Even I have seen the frenzy shown in the media clips of those last few days of evacuation from the top of the U.S. Embassy as Saigon fell to the North Vietnamese.

Once I was removed from the crash site, I was taken to the I.O.I's hospital to have my injuries addressed and then taken back to the Sacred Heart Orphanage. After about four days, we were whisked up and quickly taken to the airport for the final evacuation. With no more military planes available, a chartered Pan American Airline Boeing 747 aircraft, partially staffed with volunteering stewardesses and nurses, was sent to help in this last airlift. As I have since discovered, the last day of the Operation Babylift took out over 400 children and 60 escorts. That was the largest planeload in the effort. I have also been told that as the plane stood on the runway, the scene around the portable stairway up to the plane's door was like a fire brigade in action.

Vietnamese women and orphanage staffers hurriedly passed the babies and children to the volunteers and escorts. Those of us who had been part of the surviving "cargo" of the first plane, I was told, were crying hysterically at the sight of being loaded onto a plane once again. The remembrance of the disaster was ever so fresh in our minds, I am sure. None of the Vietnamese women—some mothers of the children departing—were allowed to enter the plane for fear of sabotage. They had to remain at the bottom of the staircase. There was no time to hesitate and no time for good-byes. While the last few of us were taken into the plane, one woman volunteer stated that there must have been about a hundred women in a circle at the bottom of the steps sobbing and waving when the door closed for take-off.

I have since read an account by one of the volunteers who

related, "I was overwhelmed as I watched the endless flow of little ones pouring into the plane filling every available space. Some were even being handed over by their mothers. Many were obviously not of full Asian bloodlines. I guessed they probably had American GI fathers. I could only wonder how many families on both sides of the Pacific were being impacted by this one planeload of children. Would we ever know what would happen to any of them?"

Our plane was headed for the San Francisco Bay Area and Travis Air Force Base. We only stopped briefly to refuel in Japan and landed on American soil within 24 hours. After landing at the air force base on a Friday, we were transferred to the Presidio military compound in San Francisco on Monday for processing. The majority of the children had already been through the adoption process and were headed for new homes. I was not one of them. Those children were moved through the process quickly and sent on to their next destination, awaiting new families. Within hours, I was to experience my next miracle.

It seems that as I was being processed, one of the personnel, upon discovering that I was not adopted, remembered a couple in Marin County—just across the Golden Gate Bridge from San Francisco—who had lost the young girl they were anticipating in that fatal crash of the first plane. For over 20 months, they had gone through the official steps and paperwork to bring her there and had been devastated by her loss. The staff person decided to pick up the phone and call the couple to see if they might be interested in me. From what I was told, my American parents received a call around 3 P.M. from the Presidio staffer who informed them that she had a little girl who was available for adoption. Since they had already been cleared, the Presidio staffer inquired whether would they be interested.

Without hesitation, they said, "Yes!"

By seven that evening, I was on my way to my new home and family.

A lot of children had been adopted in other countries such as Australia, Canada, Great Britain, and France. Although there were many of us adopted in the United States, there *was* some controversy "a-buzz." There was a rather publicized debate from some groups as to whether it was in our best interests to remove us from our homeland and ultimately deprive us of our birth culture. With the lack of documentation for many of us, concerns also arose over what might happen through the years if a parent might decide to reclaim a child. Despite this turmoil surrounding the adoptions, many others, like the couple who became my American parents, were unimpeded. For that, I am truly grateful.

Growing up in the safe and secure environment surrounded by a mother, father, and two older brothers—their biological sons—I am blessed to have the opportunity to build a wonderful life here in California, U.S.A. As I moved from childhood into adolescence and into young womanhood, I remembered little of my former life. One reason was that it seemed I had suffered some trauma-induced amnesia as a result of the plane crash. For many years, I had limited knowledge regarding where I had come from and literally knew nothing about my parents. My adoptive parents, especially my mom, have been very honest and straightforward about my adoption and felt it important that I knew as much as possible. Mom took what little identifying legal papers she had that came with me and explored other avenues, such as articles on the evacuation. Piece by piece, she began to build some wonderful scrapbooks for me to draw on for a personal foundation of *who* I am. I have those with me to this day and will use them to pass on some piece of heritage to my children.

In 1995, the agency that had worked with I.O.I. to orchestrate the adoptions of all the children brought out of Vietnam

decided to hold a 20-year reunion of the adoptees. I was notified, and my family encouraged me to go. I was surprised at
my feelings that emerged before, during, and after this gathering. So many of us with so many questions. Some still
carried much anger about what they did not know or understand about that time and the evacuation. I had worked
through much of those feelings. I was at a certain place of
peace with what I had come to accept as another lifetime and
one I would probably know very little, if anything, about—
ever. Yet there was something inside me that gave fuel to the
unanswered questions once I was with the other adoptees. The
only connections I had to my past at this particular point in
my life were the scrapbooks and the occasional voice of "Little
Loan" that would speak to me in my mind.

As a result, the agency planned a trip for the following
year so that those of us who desired could return to Vietnam
to revisit our original homeland. The thought, at first, was
overwhelming. Suddenly, we were being presented with the
opportunity to go and find what we could that would
provide answers to our birth families, our native culture, and
from where we came. None of us had ever returned to
Vietnam. My family totally supported me doing this. In fact,
my mom offered to go with me. Eighteen of us former
orphans rescued from South Vietnam decided to go.

Within months, it seemed, we were off on our journey.
Interestingly enough, the television primetime news show *48
Hours* decided to follow our return and chose me as their
focus; a presentation would be shown after our return. I had
done my homework to prepare as best I could. But upon our
arrival and during the time we were there, I was continually
awestruck by the people and the country I had known so
little about. I was able to travel up to the village in which I
was born. The route we took from Ho Chi Minh City—
formerly Saigon—was on a road that was called "The

Avenue of Terror" during the war because it had been so heavily mined. I carried with me a picture of myself at age three and some documents regarding my birth.

I wandered the streets of this small village wondering if any memory would be triggered about my childhood there. I went to what was the equivalent of a city hall to search records for any information about my mother. I found none. As I spoke to some villagers, an elderly man in a group said he thought he recognized the picture of me as a little girl and remembered that I had lived with a woman who had two children of her own. He could give no other information about me, my mother, or the whereabouts of the woman with whom I had lived. In a last ditch effort, I left my contact information at the city hall and spoke to as many people as possible who might eventually provide some information about my early life there. This was all I would find—and even that was only speculation, a *possible* answer.

Oddly enough, while I was there and walking along the waterfront, I happened to stumble upon a man bathing in the water who did not look like any of the other villagers. He resembled me more than the others; it was clear he wasn't a full-blooded Vietnamese either. When he realized that I had seen him, we locked eyes for a moment, and then he quickly retreated from the water and disappeared. For that split moment when our eyes met, there seemed to be a spark of recognition in both of us that was indescribable. I felt a rush through my body. I never saw him again during the time I was there.

We also visited the orphanage where I had been taken. Yes, it was still there. The nuns treated us like their lost children returning home. It gave me a warm feeling in my heart to see that it still stood as a monument of love and care for abandoned children. How blessed I was to have been taken there. How blessed we *all* were that these two women, Sara and Yvonne, had cared to create this haven for the outcast, discarded, and parentless. As I have mentioned, most of the half-American children who were left behind were either killed or hid in the forests, eventually moving up into the hills to survive and ultimately live. It was their only chance after the invasion of the North Vietnamese.

One of the last things I did on the trip—along with some of the others—was to visit the site of the plane crash. In my mind, I think that I just believed this was something I needed to see as one more part of this journey toward weaving together pieces of my former life. I did not expect my reaction. As I stood looking out over the rice field, still carrying the physical scars of the crash burnt onto my body, I suddenly heard the three-year-old *Little Loan* speaking in my head. Someone in the group saw me shudder and asked if I was okay. All I could say was that I needed to be alone for a moment. It suddenly became clear what I was here to do.

Tears began to well up in my eyes as I unexpectedly felt some sense of connection—however small—some particle of remembrance of that time and the tragedy of the crash. I was flooded with the sadness of those lost lives—the children who didn't make it—and the little girl from that time who had been tucked so deep inside me through all these years for protection. I felt myself exhale. It was as if I had been holding my breath all my life. As I began to take deep breaths, I felt the walls—those that had been in the making for most of my life against any memory of that little girl left behind—dissolving and running down through my body and into the ground where I stood. I knew at that moment I had done what seemed destined for me to do: Bring *Little Loan* home.

"It is done," I thought.

It was as if I was saying to that little girl who had left so many years ago, "I have brought you home. Now I can move forward with the life I have. You have come back, my little friend, to stand watch over those who didn't make it out." I lovingly blessed her as I released her to her homeland.

After my return, I did receive a letter from a woman in Vietnam who said she was the one my mother and I had lived with for a short time. I suppose I got the most information I will ever have about my mother from her letter although I will never know the accuracy of this information. I have never found anything out about my father. That may be all I ever get to know about either of my birth parents.

Miracle of miracles. When the *48 Hours* segment was shown in the U.S. after our return, the daughter-in-law of Sara, Sylvia Hopkins, recognized my story in a segment done on a national morning show and made every effort to seek me out. When we connected, Sylvia and Yvonne's daughter, Dionne, made arrangements for me to fly to the opening of the National Headquarters in Scottsdale, Arizona as a surprise to "The Ladies." I spoke as a testimony of the incredible effect their work has had on people like me. I know that if it weren't for these two women and the unselfish love, devotion, and commitment they give to children, many of us would not be here today. They took a chance many years ago to step out, speak up, and do something about abandoned and abused children. I don't know where I would be today if they hadn't been guided by some divine force to act.

I am very grateful for the family I have. They are wonderful, supportive, and we have a beautiful relationship. I have a beautiful life now, a husband of Bulgarian descent, and a precious two-year-old daughter. My husband and daughter are my primary passion. Making a positive effect regarding the rights and safety of children is one of my other passions. I am now just a year away from graduating with a law degree focused on practicing in some area of child advocacy and criminal law. I know that Sara and Yvonne's mission in life has given birth to my own. I am committed to doing what I can to care for the children who are abused, abandoned, and at risk. I have even spoken to Sara and Yvonne about doing some work with them—and for them. I'd love to devote some time to working with their children. How's that for coming full circle?

As I look back over my life and those who have had an impact on it, I will always be grateful to these two ladies who cared enough to act—to break the silence of *our* plight. Their tireless effort over the years will forever stand as a testimony of never-ending work and love. What they have created will never end. It will just continue on, and on, and on. In some unusual way, we still remain their children—here to carry on for *them*.

I thank you both from the bottom of my heart for myself and on behalf of all the children you have helped.

The numbers of children grew and grew.

Lt. General Lewis W. Walt, USMC, with orphan.

Operation Babylift: The first plane to arrive carrying babies in boxes (1975).

Sara and Yvonne with first arrivals of "Operation Babylift" out of Vietnam.

Loan (center) with Sara and Yvonne at the 1996 grand opening of Childhelp USA National Headquarters in Scottsdale, Arizona. Also pictured: (from left to right, back) Sharon Dupont, Ron Masak, Molly Beeson, Connie Stevens, Dennis James, Rhonda Fleming, Mary Hart, and Anne Jefferys.

CHAPTER THREE

bringing help home

SARA AND YVONNE LAUNCH CHILDHELP USA IN AMERICA

"You see anyone who looks familiar?" Yvonne asked me.

"Wait." I took off my gloves and pulled out a picture of a man from my coat pocket.

"See that guy just coming up the steps?" I quickly showed the picture to Yvonne and let her study it for a moment.

"Isn't that Mr. Price?"

"You're right. It is him," she said.

We had asked for an appointment several times with this man who was in charge of state licensing. But he never returned our calls, which made us all the more determined. His silence was just the catalyst we needed to inspire us to come straight to the source. So, there we were in Sacramento. Our plan was to intercept him on his way into his office and not give in until we had scored a touch-down. We were like sports figures all suited up and ready for the offense. Our bravado makes us laugh now. We went determined to see that our village would open for these younger children.

He had a quick gait, and before we knew it, he walked right up beside us. We practically had to jog to keep up with him. We'd rehearsed our lines as if we were auditioning for a part and got to the point. He didn't break a step to say "howdy," "drop dead," or anything else as he quick-stepped it up the rest of the stairs two-at-a-time, all the while getting closer and closer to his office.

We introduced ourselves and briefly reviewed the work we had done with the children in Japan, Vietnam, and Operation Babylift. We explained how many of those children have now grown to become successful adults, and we hear about them from time to time; each time we do, we cry for joy. They have become one of our many blessings.

We then gave him an overview of our Beaumont, California property and quickly told him how we were going to be the first specialized child abuse facility in America, perhaps the world. We informed him how we would have a full-time art therapist. (Nobody knew much about art therapy at the time or about using it for abused children.) We also mentioned how we planned to pioneer the use of animal therapy in child abuse treatment, which had never really been tried in such facilities. We explained to him how we planned to include the Head Start Program—which prepares disadvantaged, at risk children for kindergarten and plays a major role in child abuse prevention—in all our programs at Childhelp Village. This was because we wanted our children in residence to go with other children from the community into Head Start and that, too, would be a groundbreaking concept.

We talked fast and made our final "pitch" for the waiver to allow us to take in children under the age of six; we finished just as we reached the front door to his office.

He stopped and looked at the two of us, Yvonne and I panting from keeping up and the rapid pitch we had just made.

As we stood there, two women begging this government official who—whether he knew it at that moment—held the future in his hands of so many younger children, volunteers, and people who had trusted us with their money—we couldn't help but say a quick silent prayer.

"Your will, not ours, dear God. Your time, not ours."

After giving us both a quick once-over, Mr. Price nodded and said, "Well, I can see how determined you both are. You've obviously done your homework and understand all the problems—yours and mine. I like people like that. Why don't you go freshen up a bit, catch your breath, come back to my office in a few minutes, and we'll handle the paperwork?"

We smiled, thanked him for his courtesy, and started to walk away.

"But," he said—which stopped us dead in our tracks. What was he going to say? "I'm only going to give you the license for one year. We'll see after that."

We couldn't help ourselves and broke out into two of the giddiest looking grins you ever saw.

"That's all right," we chorused. "We completely understand. It is imperative that we get the children when they are young because we have a better chance to effect a change in their lives. These precious ones are so damaged they can't make it in foster homes most of the time. They need therapy and individual care. We'll show you the results and prove to you the importance of getting the children as young as two years old."

The Village would be the beginning for yet more miracles to take place for abused and neglected children in America.

We opened the doors of the first Childhelp Village in Beaumont, California in 1978. It was the first exclusive child abuse residential facility for two to 12-year-olds in the nation. Childhelp USA would ultimately help over 3,000,000 children through its programs from its inception to the present.

There was no turning back.

Shortly after the fall of South Vietnam and the successful completion of Operation Babylift, we were asked to speak at a luncheon at the old Ambassador Hotel in Los Angeles, California about what we had done with International Orphans, Inc. and the evacuation of children out of Vietnam. On the same podium with us were Ronald Reagan, who was running for governor at the time, and his wife, Nancy. When we spoke, we voiced that although we didn't know where this would take our lives, we felt our mission was still with children—and wherever we found a need, we would fill it.

After the program, Mrs. Reagan spoke to us about how impressed she was with the success we had had with the children of Japan and Vietnam. She then said that she would love to see us tackle the problem of child abuse in America. Needless to say, we were shocked. We had never heard there was a problem here—not many people had, if any. Mrs. Reagan was very interested in what she had heard might be an emerging problem here in the United States and hoped to see something done about it. Before we knew it, we agreed to do a feasibility study and promised that if we did find child abuse to be a problem, we would turn our efforts in that direction next. We certainly would not find child abuse issues we had seen in Japan and Vietnam here at home.

Once again, our innocence regarding child abuse was about to be fractured. Through some investigation, we stumbled onto the fact that the silent innocence of the 1950s, having been cracked wide open by the very vocal 1960s and early 1970s, had begun to give a voice to the secret plight of children in America, which we clearly understood as child abuse. The horror of what child abuse encompassed in our homeland took our breath away, and we realized this must be what God had in mind for us to do next. It was time to break the silence at home. It was time to bring our efforts home.

What we uncovered astonished us. We didn't realize what our research and reports would expose and bring to light what was going on behind the doors of America. The more questions we asked, the more people began to speak out. We had learned much about the "abandoned child" through our work overseas. But we would unfortunately have that knowledge expanded by our discovery of the neglect, plus the physical, emotional, and sexual abuse that was happening to children at home. It was unbelievable to us that this problem had been swept "under the rug" all this time.

Immediately, we could see the need to build a facility for children who suffered abuse—a place of refuge, a respite, where the needs of these unfortunate children became the sole focus of an established village for safety and healing. Yvonne and I decided to do what we knew how to do— speak out. Sometimes the easiest way to break the silence is to open your mouth and just ask for what you need. Once again, the calls went out, and we staged a big party to serve as a fundraiser at Yvonne's home. We were ready to step out and describe this dilemma to our community of friends and acquaintances.

The scheduled fundraiser occurred, and we were surprised at the turnout—around 700. The event went well throughout the evening, and then it came time for us to address the gathering. After reiterating what we had been doing abroad, we explained what we had found going on at home. We shared some of the stories from our hearts, and then proceeded to lay our proposal before our audience.

The next thing I remember is Yvonne saying, "What we need now is property to create this Village."

Then one guest, Nat Dumont, stood up, and announced, "I own property in Beaumont, California. I would be willing to donate 20 acres. Let's do this."

We were thrilled but turned to each other during the applause from the audience with a look that said, "Where is Beaumont, California?"

Neither of us had ever heard of it. The evening continued, and we were awe-struck at the compassionate response we received from most in attendance. We were on our way. As it turned out, this wonderful man gave us 20 acres that evening, and every time we had another fundraiser, he gave us more property in Beaumont, California (near Palm Springs), which eventually totaled 120 acres.

Although we had full architectural and site plans drawn up underwritten by a friend of Yvonne's husband as a gift, it was the year building costs underwent four major increases. By the time we had enough money to begin phase one, the actual construction costs went outside our budget. We then raised more money. But the costs rose once again, which then tripled and quadrupled. We already owned all that land, yet the dramatic rise in building costs made it impossible for us to start. Although we became extremely frustrated, the powerful hand of God came into play once again.

Out of the clear blue sky, the San Diego Catholic Diocese called us one day and said, "We're about to sell our San Diego Boy's Town property in Beaumont, and we understand it touches on your present property where you are planning to build. Perhaps you would like to take a look at our establishment?"

We convinced a group of men, including builders and our husbands, to go down with us to look the property over, and give us their feedback. It was large. And even if its existing buildings needed extensive repairs, we'd still be considerably ahead of our development schedule if we bought the property. We had originally planned to build in several phases over two to five years on the property we already owned.

The diocese wanted over $4 million for the property, and we had no way of meeting their asking price. Yet our team was unanimous.

"It's a steal at $4.5 million," they agreed.

What were we to do? We didn't have anywhere near the $4.5 million, but we wanted the property because we knew it would jump-start our whole program here in the U.S. We could only scrape up enough money to offer $1.8 million—and most of that was in pledges. We didn't actually have the cash in hand, yet we felt strongly that this is what we were to do.

We told one of our support team who was an avowed atheist that we planned to step out in faith and offer the diocese all the $1.8 million we had.

He laughed. "That's almost embarrassing," he remarked. "The $4.5 million is a tremendous price for that property, and your offer will be a huge slap in the face."

We looked at each other. What else could we do—we didn't have the money.

In jest, this same man said, "I'll tell you what: If they accept your price, I'll believe in God."

We stood firm and said we were going to give it a try.

The day of the big meeting finally came. We took our team along and went down to the offices of the diocese. Most of our experts believed they would have to negotiate and try to pick up the pieces of the deal after the diocese turned us down. They had rehearsed the negotiation and created plan "B" and plan "C."

After a little chitchat, we came to the point.

"All we can offer is $1.8 million," we told him.

I can't believe how gutsy we were. Our attorneys were embarrassed for us—and themselves. A long silence ensued. It seemed like five minutes passed, but, of course, it wasn't that long. Everybody else squirmed, or looked down at their feet, or gazed out the windows at the beautiful view of Mission Bay. We just stared back across the table without batting an eye at the bishop and several monsignors who were in charge.

We'll never forget the bishop's clear, penetrating blue eyes. He didn't bat an eye either, which just peered a hole right through us. We didn't know how he was going to react—what he was going to say or whether he would be mad.

We just kept thinking, "If this be His will . . ."

Finally, after a silence that seemed an eternity, the bishop cleared his throat.

"I think we can manage that," he stated with a smile.

Everybody on our side of the table nearly fell out of their chair. We couldn't believe our ears, and were beside ourselves with joy. At that moment, in the midst of utter joy as Yvonne and I were celebrating our triumph, we froze as we suddenly realized that if we paid them all our money right away, we wouldn't have a dime left to meet payroll, or buy paint, or spend on anything. We turned and courageously explained our situation to the good bishop; he couldn't have been more gracious. He worked out a deal with us wherein we gave him all our money, except for approximately $100,000, and he would give us extra time to go out and raise that money.

We walked out of that meeting ecstatic. Another obstacle met by a miracle. Our child abuse village was on its way in America. God heard our prayers and knew we were doing it for His glory.

Oh, yes, and true to his word, our atheist member of the team became a believer.

After moving through some additional obstacles, the Village became ours. We signed the papers on New Year's Eve 1976 and then took one entire year to renovate the buildings. Every single volunteer we could beg, borrow, or sweet-talk, including our own families, spent his or her weekends and holidays with us. In fact, our own children, John, Chuck, Brian, and Dionne took their Easter break to help paint; we all slept on the floor. Volunteers from a nearby military base, schools, churches—you name it—all showed up. And we weren't bashful about asking for help either; there was a ton of work to do, and we didn't have any money to pay—so we begged a lot.

Merely locating staff was a big problem because colleges and universities didn't even teach about child abuse in those days. Thus, we decided to educate and create our own experts somehow. We had to have a whole complement of staff, including social workers, teachers, an all-faiths chaplain, caregivers, medical staff, therapists, counselors, a chef, maintenance people, and so forth. Everybody needed to be on board before the licensing professionals would even consider our facility ready for our first child. The children wouldn't all come at once. We would have one child, and then maybe two children, and then maybe five children, and so on and so forth until we had a full complement—up to 80.

The biggest problem would be the state licensing. Because there had never been a facility like ours in the United States—one whose only expertise was dealing with child abuse and victims—who were the only kind of children we would take—all the government agencies we contacted were a little puzzled about how to deal with us.

From this realization, we got the idea that if we worked at trying to take in the younger children—the ones who could not adjust in foster homes—we could show a significant improvement a lot more quickly, thus getting their lives off on the right foot sooner. But at that time, a California law precluded us from accepting children under six years of age because it was considered institutionalizing such a young child. Yet we were determined to rescue the younger children.

Everyone said, "Oh, you'll never get them because the state won't allow it."

Yvonne and I looked at each other.

"Want to bet?" we challenged.

We chorused without saying a prior word to each other. After so many years of working together, we could pretty much read each other's mind once we were in the same room. There were even lots of times when we could read each other's mind when we were miles and miles apart. But that's another story.

As you know, we did open our Village and were also able to take in the younger children. We had wonderful press coverage with over 2,000 people in attendance—the governor, the Director of the Department of Health and Human Services in Washington, D.C., senators, congressmen, volunteers, and friends. The press coverage only helped bring our mission to the eyes and ears of more people as we launched the first residential center in the world strictly focused on abused children.

A wonderful side note about the opening of the Beaumont Village involved Mama Kin and the children of the Japanese orphanage. When they heard we were opening our first orphanage here at home, Mama Kin and the children baked cookies and sold them on the streets of Tokyo to raise money to support us. The funds totaled almost $5,000. Amazing—and from cookies! That is love. They wanted to express their gratefulness to us. Since we had helped them in their time of need, they wanted to help us with our mission here in return.

lisa's story

ALL WHO ENTER HERE WILL FIND LOVE

My name is Lisa. It seems so long ago, like another world, and another lifetime. But I can vividly remember arriving at the Village, frightened, and wondering why I had been taken from the foster home where I had been with my two sisters. What had I done that was so bad? Why were these people separating us? And what was this huge place I had been taken to that had this sign over the door that read, "All who enter here will find love"? I'd seen that type of sign or heard those words before—usually at places I'd been kicked out of. This surely wasn't going to last.

I was ten and had been living with my sisters in our third "family home" in two years. I didn't think I had done anything wrong by wanting to be alone most of the time, and I didn't like being made to do things I didn't want to do. The family would get upset with me about that, and would say I was difficult and resistant about following directions. Well, the problem was that they just always told me what to do. Every time I would ask, "Why do I have to?" I would be punished for talking back. So, I spent a lot of time in my room. My sisters were better at it. They learned well living at the home before we were taken away by the social workers. We had been taught to keep our mouths shut—no matter what.

The family said I was just not working out but that they would keep my sisters. So, here I was being brought to this huge place with a lot of people asking questions and "checking me out." There were doctors, nurses, case-workers, a chaplain, and later I would meet a woman known as the "Art Lady." I tried to explain that I needed to know why I was being asked to do something I didn't want to do, and I also didn't like it when one of the adults at the home I had come from wanted to hold me or hug me. If they started that and didn't stop when I told them to, I would usually start hitting. At that time, I wasn't able to explain why. I don't really think I understood it then.

When we lived with my biological parents before being taken away, it was rough and rocky. My mom and dad would fight a lot, and it most often ended up with them knocking each other around. My sisters and I would get so scared that we would hide in the closet until it was over. I would wrap a blanket around the two of them and get them to hide as far back in the closet as possible; I am the oldest, and I wanted to protect them. Sometimes I would go back out into the room and try to get my parents to stop fighting, and they would end up hitting me. So, I learned not to do that and just let them go at it until it was over. Only when they started throwing things or it got so loud was I afraid that the neighbors were going to call the cops one more time. I guess they really didn't like each other. The closet became our protector—and a few times, my prison.

My mom worked at the local K-Mart to help put food on the table and get the rent paid because my dad rarely worked. We barely had enough to get by. My middle sister and I would go to school during the day, and so we would have to leave my little sister at home with my dad. I hated that. When we came home, he was usually passed out on the sofa. I would have to start dinner, and my other sister would feed something to our little sister because she usually hadn't been fed the whole day. Lots of times, she would have to be bathed because she had messed her clothes. She was only two.

When my mom would come home, we would eat, and she and dad would start in drinking. Before long, they would be at it again—shouting, cursing, and sometimes chasing each other around the house with things while threatening to kill each other. All my sisters and I wanted to do was stay out of the way until it was over. Most of the time, my dad would end it all by grabbing his jacket and walking out the door. I now think he started a lot of the fights to find an excuse to get out of the house. We would be left with our mom who had no interest in finding out about our day. We were just supposed to leave her alone.

I remember one evening when my dad had left, my mom asked me to go to the kitchen and get her another beer. I was paralyzed with fear, knowing what was going to happen if she kept drinking. When I didn't move, she came and grabbed me by the arm, and pulled me to the bathroom. She plugged the tub and turned the water on. The *hot* water. She told me to get into the tub—clothes and all. I begged her not to make me. She picked me up and threw me down into the hot water.

As I sat there crying with the water getting hotter and hotter and higher and higher, all she said to me was, "Feel that heat? That is only a hint of how hot it's going to get if you ever refuse to do what I tell you to again."

She made me stay in that tub the whole night.

It was hard getting up and going to school everyday. We never brought any of our friends home because we didn't know what would be going on with my dad. A lot of times when we got home, he would have some of his buddies there, and they had been drinking and doing drugs all day. I also didn't like it because when they were there, he would make me play "waitress" for them. I didn't like being in the room with them because they were nasty and talked about things I didn't want to hear about.

There were those nights when my father had been out after a fight with my mom when I would hear him fly into the driveway in the car and come to a screeching halt that sounded like the car was coming through the wall. I would begin to shake in the bed. My mom would be asleep on the sofa with the TV going loudly, and my sisters were also asleep in the bed we shared in another room. I would listen closely to hear if Dad would just come in and go to bed. That is what I hoped for. On some nights, he would go in and try to wake up my mother and get her to come to bed. And often, she would refuse, telling him to leave her alone.

Those were my nights of horror.

A lot of the time on those kinds of nights, he would come into our room, pull me out of the bed, and take me to his bedroom. I slept on the outside because of this, keeping my sisters toward the wall. I knew what those nights were going to be about. He would take me to his room and then do things to me or make me do things to him all the while saying, "Your mommy doesn't understand me," or "I am doing this because I love you," or "Do you know you are Daddy's 'special little girl?'" All I knew was that some of it hurt, or it was ugly. If this was "love," I wanted no part of it. And I certainly didn't want to be anyone's "special little girl" if this was what happened.

A couple of times, I tried to cry out or tell my mom.

That's when my dad would say I was lying and locked me in the closet for days at a time. I actually didn't mind it much except for not getting out to go to the bathroom. My middle sister would get up at night and try to push any food she could under the door.

Eventually, my dad got arrested for robbing a 7-Eleven and had to go to prison. It was really embarrassing for us at school, and my mom lost her job over it. Then we were left with no way to pay bills or get food. My mom just began to drink more and started bringing strange men home. She would come in with them, and they would bring all this food. Most of the time they would just leave the food for us and just drink before going to her room. Maybe bringing food home for us was why she did it. It wasn't long before the county social workers came to our house. A neighbor had called them about what was going on. By that time, my sister and I rarely went to school. We had to take care of Mom and the house. They sent Mom to a shelter. And we were off to begin our merry-go-round rides of one house to another, one family to another for the next couple of years.

After many weeks of being at Childhelp Village, I started to let my guard down. I missed my sisters but got to talk to them on the phone a couple of times a week. The foster family even said that if I got "straightened out," they might consider taking me back. The people at the Village were really nice and seemed to care. The thing I liked most was that they asked me if I wanted to do something. And if I asked "why," they would try to explain the reason. They also seemed to understand that I didn't want anyone touching me or trying to hug me. I would later find out that was about having boundaries.

Within the first month, I got to go to a place that they called the "ranch." I liked it there because there was this dog without one ear that would come right up to me every time

I went. I felt like he knew what it was like to be hurt. I never found out how he lost his ear, but we always had fun together. When I would ride one of the white ponies, he would just follow along like he had known me for a long time. Each time I went, it was like he knew I was coming and was waiting for me.

For the first week, I didn't sleep much because I wondered if someone was going to come into the room to take me away. I really didn't trust anyone at that point. Then on the second week, they gave me a new bike. I had never had anything like that before. The food was good, and we had breakfast, lunch, and dinner. And you could eat as much as you wanted. I didn't have to share mine with anybody like it had been at home when we had so little. I got new clothes and this beautiful new dress for Sundays. It made me feel happy to wear it. One of the cottage workers told me I looked pretty.

I would hear some of the other children talking to each other about what life had been like before they got there and started to realize some bad things had happened to other children also. Not just me. Yet I wasn't ready to talk about my home. It was too painful. Pretty soon, this girl in my cottage and I started to be friends. She would ask me if I wanted to do things with her. We made a promise to meet each day when we returned from school and do stuff together. I had never had a friend before.

I think it was at about the end of the first month that I was there when one day this lady came to the cottage to meet me. I found out by talking to her that they called her the "Art Lady." We talked for a while, and she told me about this room she had that was full of fun things to do. You could draw, play music and dance, play dress-up, write poems, play with the stuffed animals, or just sit and talk. She asked if I would like to visit sometime. There was something about her that I liked instantly. Her voice was soft, and she had a nice smile. I looked forward to going.

Once I started going with the Art Lady to the room she had, it became one of my favorite things to do. Sometimes we would just clean up from when all the other children had been there and talk. Sometimes we would draw, and she taught me how to write poems. I like to write. I think it is neat how you can tell stories by writing and making them up. I also like to draw, and we would just sit and draw pictures then show them to each other. I remember at first that most of my pictures were sad to me. I would draw my sisters and me, people trying to take them away, and lots of rain clouds. Sometimes I would draw my parents fighting.

Then one day while we were looking at our drawings together, the Art Lady told me: "You must have had a really tough time when you were at home."

Well, I just broke down and started to cry. Could she really know what I had been through? And you know what? She just let me cry and didn't tell me to stop.

I was really glad that it had only been the two of us there that afternoon. After that, and over the next weeks and months, I began to tell her everything that went on at my home and how I missed my sisters. I even told her about those nights my dad would come get me and take me to his room. Sometimes we cried together. She became my first adult friend. I knew I could trust her. One day when I was there, she asked me to draw a picture of what I would like things to be. When I was finished, she asked to put it up on the wall.

I answered, "Yes."

I felt proud of that picture because she asked to hang it up. It had this big bright sun shining down on my sisters and me. I also learned how to write more things with her and got better at it. I like writing, and maybe someday will write about my life. She thinks I am good.

I am 19 now and live on my own. I have a job, attend community college at nights, and visit my sisters often. A lot happened for me at Childhelp Village. I began to learn how to trust and how to believe in myself. I learned things that I am good at. And I learned how to deal with my anger and sadness. I know now that I am not the only kid whom bad things happened to, and that most of the time, it had nothing to do with me. Some people just have a hard time with their lives. Like my parents. We don't really hear from my mother these days. My dad writes, and says that when he gets out of prison, he wants to come, get my sisters and me, and take care of us. I also have come to understand that that probably won't happen.

I think I can have a good life ahead. I learned that the people at the Village really did care about me, and some of them I believe really loved me—like the Art Lady. I did find out a different meaning for love while I was there. I call my friend, the Art Lady, when I can, just to say "hello." I miss her but am happy that we stay in contact. I will never forget her, and I know she won't forget me. When I left, she made sure to come see me to say goodbye.

When it was time to go, she stepped up to me, gave me a big hug, and said, "You are my special girl."

And for the first time, it felt good to hear that.

a special friend's story

A CONNECTION FOREVER

*I*n the fall of 1990, I was given the name of a young boy at one of the residential villages who did not yet have a "Special Friend." When the time came to meet him as his new Special Friends, both my husband and I were excited and nervous. We had never served as mentors to anyone before. At Halloween, his first holiday at the Village, we decided to send him a costume as an initial connection so he could be part of his first party in the residence. We also thought this would help him know that someone was thinking of him especially since we hadn't met yet.

Traditionally, Christmas brings the children's Christmas pageant and Santa Claus to each Village. For us, it would be our first meeting with him and we were hopeful for a quick bonding. In an effort to boost our initial meeting and to enhance the connection, we persuaded our nephew, who was 21 at the time, to be with us at the Christmas celebration. Unfortunately, we were not as successful as we had hoped to be. I think there have been too many strangers at one time.

Our Special Friend was very withdrawn and making conversation was very limiting. Also, he was disappointed in our choice of gift, a telescope, which we had understood he was eager to have. Yet we made it through the party, Santa's arrival, and the rest of the day together, holding hope in our hearts. Afterward, we still were committed, and agreed to give it another try.

Our next meeting was on his birthday in the middle of January 1991. He had elected—one of the *gifts* the children are given—to have his party at Chuck E. Cheese's. We had a very nice day as we celebrated his eighth birthday and parted really encouraged. Over the rest of the year, we had many visits, all of which made us feel wonderful about this budding relationship. We were invited and attended all his soccer games, including the playoff games. We were also invited to his next birthday, which took place in a nearby park—fun times with a special meaning. The occasions and memories began to build and grow amongst us.

Two months after his ninth birthday, we were told he was being moved to one of Childhelp's group homes in Orange County, California. It was really a sad day for us when we had to say farewell. The farewell party was on a Sunday, and he left armed with stamped envelopes to write us, as well as other parting gifts. At this point, contact with the boy was put on hold as the "Special Friends" program at that time did not extend outward to the group homes. All of our contact was by mail, with cards for specific occasions, birthday presents, and Christmas gifts.

To our excitement, approximately a year and a half later, the rules were changed and we were able to have direct contact once again. From that time forward, there followed many visits and lots of fun outings of movies, miniature golf, lunches, and mall shopping. As his "family," we attended his grade school graduation and met with his teachers to discuss his progress and needs for the next level. A short time later, he was moved from the group home environment and was placed in one of Childhelp's foster care homes with a wonderful family. We were very proud of him because to move into foster care is a step up for any child from the Village. During that time, with their permission, we continued to maintain an interaction with him. The placement with that family lasted nearly a year. He was then placed with another Childhelp foster family, and we were able to once again stay connected with the family's permission.

The teenage years brought about a wonderful collection of times together as we attended his basketball and soccer games. Over the years, he has been a visitor to our home. We have had field trips to Magic Mountain, Universal Studios, and Knott's Berry Farm. Woven through the years were long conversations regarding the need for maintaining grades for his future entrance into college.

During his high school years, his foster family adopted him. His new father was an Elder in their church. As a result, the teenage boy became heavily involved in the youth programs of the church.

The time finally arrived for graduation from high school, and we were excited to be invited to be a part of that special day. It was a wonderful evening with his family and young friends. We felt very proud to have been a part of the growth of this young man who had been initially rescued by Childhelp. Our long conversations and the seeds we had planted are quite visibly germinating. He now attends a community college and is part of the basketball team. He is majoring in drama and is pursuing a career in entertainment. He is a very good-looking young man who tops out at 6'3".

Due to his busy schedule these days, our contacts are not as frequent as they once were. Yet we continue to connect on birthdays and holidays, which is a big treat for us all. We are committed to staying in touch and get periodic updates on school, his new car, basketball games, or whatever else is important at the time. Phone calls still end with "love you both," and our response always is, "Love you, too."

Even though we have had other Special Friends from Childhelp Village, our involvement in our first one's life has always remained steadfast. The reward has been tremendous. Knowing that we have had some impact on a young life has made all the round trips to wherever he was worthwhile. He, and the program Childhelp created, has most assuredly had an impact on our lives—a wonderful one. Thank you!

First Childhelp USA residential village, Beaumont, California.

Entrance to Childhelp Village West (Beaumont, California).

Yvonne and Sara visiting
children at Childhelp Village West.

Yvonne and Sara with children
at a Childhelp USA residential village.

Nancy Reagan with Yvonne and Sara at the Humanitarian
Awards Luncheon (May 2003).

Rhonda Fleming Chapel at Childhelp Village West.

deadline 3 p.m.

CHILDHELP USA EXPANDS TO THE EAST COAST

"*I*'m the bad seed."

Our hearts sank when we heard this. There she was, a little girl not more than eight years old, and those were the first words out of her mouth when she came to the Culpeper, Virginia Village. Not even a "hello."

The children who come to the Villages, really, for the most part, have been victimized badly and with such repetition that they feel what has happened to them is their fault. They think this wouldn't be happening to them if they only were "good" children. This is typical of the abused child. As a result, every time they go out and see families or watch families on TV who are having interactions that they perceive are "normal" or "good," and every time they observe a mom or dad show up at school to bring cupcakes for their child's birthday, a little bell goes off in their head. And that bell signals to the child: "I'm a bad kid."

Stories like this have served to affirm, and at the same time reinforce, our passionate mission to continue creating as many villages and advocacy centers as we can possibly manage across the country.

As the Beaumont Village began to grow, we found ourselves stepping out of California more and more to spread the message, *and vision*, of Childhelp Villages to points beyond in the U.S. We were regularly building chapters throughout the nation and speaking in Washington on behalf of abused children.

We soon realized that there would be great value in having a Village near the nation's capital. It would be invaluable because interested people had to fly from Washington to California constantly to see what we were doing—congressmen, senators, and various other people for legislation we were trying to put through. People really didn't understand the *Village* concept until they saw it. We also began to feel that every state in the United States could use a village.

There wasn't one state we didn't go to that didn't say, "You'd be our knights in shining armor because we've needed this for so long."

It was as if the world was our oyster, asking us to come and create this pearl. It seemed like we just had to be guided where to go next. Sara and I had been led from the beginning when we opened the one in California. It finally became clear to us that there would be at least four villages—North, South, East, and West. By having a village in these four points of the U.S., people could have easier access to visit and see what we were doing. We felt they would serve as models for what might be done in their communities. Even if they couldn't recreate exactly what we had done, it would give them incentive to look at programs on a scale they could manage.

We knew the second one would be near Washington, D.C. We would start with a chapter. They would learn the history of Childhelp, then we would make arrangements for them to come to the Beaumont Village to see, first hand, how we operated. Once they were "on board," we would send them out into the community to promote the concept. While that was progressing, Sara and I, along with our staff and professional aides, would do a feasibility study as our homework. Our objective going into the community would be to see what programs were needed and what it would take to make it happen. Upon doing our study in Washington, D.C., we found there *was* a tremendous need for a village and advocacy center. This did not surprise us, yet we felt the village should be outside of the district. First of all, you couldn't get enough property inside D.C. Second, it would better serve the children in need from all the immediate surrounding areas—D.C., Virginia, and Maryland.

We started a chapter, which quickly gained momentum, and put a lady we met there in charge as Acting Director. We were being underwritten, so we were able to give her offices and secretarial backup for support. It soon became obvious to our lady in charge that this project had strong potential, was growing in recognition, and was having a strong impact around the area. But along the way, she began to feed the chapter erroneous information. She told them that we are California-based and would just take their money and run back home, never giving them any voice in governing their own region. The doubt took hold and began to spread.

Without our knowledge, she initiated a campaign to launch her own centers with her at the helm. It was naïve of us, but we had no clue of this until it turned into a huge ripple effect. She managed to do a wonderful job shooting holes through Childhelp and our integrity by convincing a great deal of the participants that we were not really going to do what we said we were.

She presented her information by asserting, "Since I am on the 'inside' of this organization, I can tell you what I see going on," and then urged them to reconsider carefully being a part of the project.

What she did was very diabolical and tore the group apart. It was only when we came back to an event that we realized what was going on. There were some people who knew of us, but most people didn't know us personally. They had been drawn to our project by our enthusiasm. Most people when faced with controversy think, "Well, I'm not going to get into this debacle," and just walk away. By the time we found all this out, it was too late. The damage was done. We had to start from ground zero with the intention this time of establishing much more involvement. That was a huge lesson learned early on in the evolution of Childhelp.

In the midst of all this upheaval with our group in the East, we had found the perfect property for the Village in the Virginia countryside. The current owners explained how it originally had been built by a father for his handicapped child and the care of numerous other handicapped children. In other words, the father of the handicapped child had built this place that was like a residential center to be shared by children who were disadvantaged like his son. He had wanted his son, and others like him, to be together and not feel different. What an act of love this had been. The buildings there were great, and the present owners had purchased the property and turned it into a breeding farm for gorgeous show horses. They had constructed a mammoth indoor riding ring and fabulous stables. The whole place was just unbelievably beautiful and well maintained. Of course, it was just out of this world for our equestrian program. It was 260 acres of the most gorgeous rolling hills with white fencing everywhere, and it included a private chapel. Were we in the right place or what? We knew we still would have to build residential treatment facilities, but we could make do with the existing buildings and phase those in.

As we found this property, we had already begun trying to re-establish another chapter there. Some of the people who had been in the initial chapter eventually realized what untruths had been told about us and our organization, and returned willing to give another try. However, to get more people involved, we realized we were going to have to get the Village initialized before people were to believe that we were sincerely honest about what we were proclaiming regarding the plans of our organization. The former "managing president" had done her damage.

Sara and I looked at each other once again and agreed, "Let's make it happen!"

There was a lady we knew back in California who had been a wonderful friend to us and to Childhelp USA. Her name was Alice C. Tyler, and her husband was co-founder of Farmers Insurance Group. Alice had played a great role financially in bringing about the Village in Beaumont. She had seen how hard we'd worked trying to get the one in the D.C. area off the ground.

She had said to Sara at one point: "You look so tired. This thing in Virginia, getting it up and started, is going to kill you."

And Sara replied, "Well, I guess it would be worth it," kind of jokingly.

Alice was not well and was in the hospital around Christmas when she called our home on Christmas day and said, "Yvonne, get Sara on the phone. I want you both on the phone when I tell you what I am going to give you for Christmas." I quickly called Sara to the phone and told Alice: "Okay, we're both here."

"Ladies, I have been with one of my attorneys all day, and I'm giving you the money to buy the property in Virginia."

"Praise God," we gulped.

We just couldn't believe what we had heard. We were thrilled. Once again, someone who had watched us walking through our obstacles and heartaches around our efforts to establish a residential center on the East Coast for our children stepped forward in support. Later, we would also find out that Alice had been intrigued that the place we wanted to purchase in Virginia was $1.8 million. She had remembered we had gotten the Beaumont property for the same exact amount and thought to herself that something very "right" was going on with us—serendipitous—a spiritual connection to something larger. With that knowledge, she felt she had to be a part of it.

Of course, we were elated and immediately began to negotiate with the lawyers and the owner of the property to make the purchase. When Alice had made her decision in the hospital, she spoke with one of the attorneys with whom she usually dealt, and all was well. Now entered the rest of the attorneys from the firm who handled her estate who had not been present when she had offered the gift to us, and they were less than enthusiastic about her decision. It seemed they wanted her money for charitable endeavors to remain in California in programs that they were directly involved wherein they could enjoy personal recognition.

We were inundated with a series of roadblocks that were mind-boggling for us to hurdle in order to receive Alice's gift. One roadblock was that they didn't want any structures we proposed to build to have Alice Tyler's name on them unless they approved what they were going to look like when finished. As a result, we had to pay an architect to do a rendering of each building we proposed to build, and, of course, that evolved into a site plan. Then came the request for an environmental impact study— Alice was very much into saving the environment. That was something we were already aware of.

After that was completed, we heard, "Well, the property may have passed and proven to be environmentally sound, but we don't know about the neighbors. They could object to having something like this in their area. We should do a study."

So, next we had to do a community impact study from all the surrounding farms, neighbors, and town.

Next, we were informed, "Well, you know that area is very ripe right now, and the railroad might come through it."

This was an obvious test to our faith—and patience. We just kept putting one foot in front of the other having faith it would all work out.

Having had so many of our obstacles turn into miracles, Sara and I took another leap of faith signing the papers and giving a down payment to hold the property for 60 days until all these studies had been done. Before long, we finally had gotten through everything that was thrown at us and stood facing one challenge left to conquer. We had to get the town supervisors of Culpeper, Virginia, where the Village was to be located, to sign off on agreement for us to operate our residential center. Everything else had been done.

We had begun to know one of the supervisors quite well through all the studies we had gone through for Alice's attorney. He was a very nice country gentleman.

When we contacted him about getting the approval he told us: "Well, I'll tell ya. I can't get in touch with one of the supervisors. He is off with his relatives somewhere, and I don't even know how or where to reach him. We only meet twice a year, and you know it's in-between meetings and everybody's gone."

We were not about to give up at this point, so we kept insisting, "But this is so important."

He replied, "Ladies, I understand. But I don't think there's a prayer of locating him in time for your deadline. I've had a heck of a time getting in touch with the others."

"But we're going to lose the property if you don't help us."

"I'll do my very best, but I can't promise you."

"Well, it has to be completed by 3 P.M. next Monday afternoon. That's all the time we've been allowed in order to keep the *seed money*. After that, we will have to forfeit everything."

We were anxious all weekend, and the only thing we could do was pray about it. And we prayed constantly. After a weekend that seemed to last years, Monday morning finally arrived. When we called, we were told that his efforts to contact the remaining voter had still not been successful. We felt as if we were up against a brick wall. How could we come through so much and be so close and then lose this property?

"Well, we have to go to the appointment in a few hours with the owner, his lawyer, and ours. We'll be in the owner's attorney's office by 1:30 P.M., so let me give you the phone and fax numbers in case you get anything by then," Sara told the gentleman.

The owner of the property knew that if our deal fell through, he would have all these studies that had been done with our money, as well as our good-faith deposit. He would only be benefited and in a better position for any future sales opportunities. When we arrived, we could see that it was hard for him not to be a bit joyful. As we sat there silently praying for that all-important phone call, Sara and I were beginning to drop into a place of sadness in the midst of the deafening silence of the room. We felt drained and heartsick over the possibility of everything we had worked for being lost. It was now seven minutes until three, and we felt all hope that we would hear from the head supervisor going out the window.

All of a sudden, the silence was broken as we heard a ring. Everyone's posture shot straight up in our chairs, as heads and eyes turned to focus in the direction of the sound. The fax machine clicked and then began to print. Sara and I looked at each other. Could it be? We grabbed hands and held our breath. As the owner's attorney slowly got up and moved toward the machine—we wanted him to run—we held our breath as we watched him reading.

He shook his head and then announced, "Well, well, ladies, it looks like you have a unanimous vote to go ahead."

I looked at the clock as it hit *exactly* 3 P.M.

"Thank you, God," we both chimed.

The property was ours, and the National Board of Directors voted to raise the money—and the Childhelp Village in the East was born.

We forged ahead with no initial subsidy. But once the word was out that we had the property, the funding literally began coming from people all over the United States. It had ignited out of the embers. Yet we had to get out there and work quickly. Learning from our past experience, we sent a man out as the director that had worked at the Village in California this time. He headed our residential treatment center there, and we joyously advanced him to the director of this Village. He knew the philosophy of Childhelp and its inner workings. He had been in our Village in California as a caregiver, had gone back to school to get his masters degree, and continued to work for Childhelp as Director of Residential Services all that time. Because he had been with us for so long, we had a working relationship already in place. We trusted him.

As a director, he worked at putting everything together with staff and so forth, while we kept busy raising the money. We had to refurbish some of the buildings to make them livable. Then people around Virginia, Maryland, and D.C. started coming out to see the facility. They loved it and many jumped right in to help us get it open. Our chapter in that area is now one of the strongest groups we have. They have raised so much funding through their successful events to the point where we have been able to build a completely new building each year since we have opened.

It's a beautiful, beautiful site. We named it the Alice C. Tyler Village of Childhelp East—serving children and the environment. Dear Alice died shortly after we got the property and never got to see it completed. Even though she told us she had left us in the will for an endowment, we have never received anything. Unfortunately, you know, those things happen sometimes. She loved what we were doing, and we loved her, so we just moved forward—one step at a time in Virginia—and decided to name the Village after Alice. We knew she wanted to be a part of this in some way, just as she had been with our Village in California. Our desire was to honor this woman for what she had done to support us in the beginning. She was such an extraordinary human being, and the decision was an easy one.

We opened officially in 1993, and our First Lady, Barbara Bush, dedicated our Village East.

We often think how close we came to not getting that property. We just kept praying the weekend before the final meeting. We had many roadblocks put in front of us, but we knew it was right. We knew prayer is stronger than any obstacles, and we just kept praying. We think about sitting there in the office that Monday afternoon trying to stay as positive as we could with the deadline minutes away. We kept saying to the owner that some way it was going to work out. And, of course, it did. God was at the core of *this* mission. How could it not happen?

We are very proud of our Village in Virginia, emulated from our Village in California. All of our villages do magnificent work. All involved have been very successful with their outreach programs. The staff is good in all areas. They have won practically every award there is for doing what they do for children. We are blessed to have people working with us who excel at what they do; they are outstanding and dedicated.

There is no doubt in our minds that God is in charge here.

dustin's breakthrough

A CHILDHELP THERAPIST SHARES HER STORY

Here's a story about a young man who at first appeared beyond hope. I'll call him "Dustin." He was born in South Central Los Angeles to a Caucasian mother and an African-American father. Things did not go well from the first day of his life. His parents were not married, and his mother would take him and disappear for periods of time with other men. The mother pretty much ignored the boy, just dragged Dustin wherever she could go to get her next "fix"—whatever that happened to be. It was hard for the father to keep up with where they were in order to take care of his son.

From meetings and case study, it was obvious the boy had a very unhealthy family system going. Within four days of birth, the child was in the hospital for some sort of infection that most children get taken care of automatically. And he almost died from it. At that point, his maternal grandfather stepped in and started to take control over the care of the child. His choice was to focus on telling his daughter how she was to raise the child, and not on her addictions, which brought about the neglect—typical pattern for someone who chooses to remain in denial.

Through all the abuse and intermittent involvement with his mother and grandfather, Dustin was in and out of foster and group homes too many times to count. A lot of the details of the mom's involvement in his abuse were locked away in the boy's subconscious because he desperately needed to stay attached to his mother. Who else did he have? He certainly had reasons to be confused and suffer from issues of abandonment.

When I first met Dustin, I was standing in the kitchen of one of the village cottages after making a cup of tea, and he was sitting at the kitchen counter. I said "hello" to which I received no response. He wouldn't make eye contact.

After a moment of complete silence I said, "So, what is your name? Mine is Helen."

All of a sudden, without a word, he began to crawl around on the floor, then stood up on chairs, next jumped around like on a pogo stick, and finally ended up on the top of the counter curled up in a ball. All this and he never said a word. That was my initial meeting with Dustin. He weighed about 100 pounds, and stood about 4'10"—a big boy for his age. He has beautiful cocoa-colored skin, an Afro, and huge beautiful eyes and eyelashes that could just melt your heart by the sadness you saw behind them.

Suddenly Dustin was like a meteor—flashing all over the place. He had a grin on his face that was more of a grimace, something I see a lot with such boys—smiles that look more like pain. He seemed to have a sort of inner charge—anxious, stressed, bewildered, and desperate. It was as if he'd just dropped in on us from outer space somewhere. It took us a long time to piece together the details of his history.

When he first arrived, he started off tearing up the

cottage where he lived. He would do everything he could to get the house stirred up, uptight, and riled-up. The minute the house was calm, he would start agitating and provoking. He had to have chaos all around him.

This kind of behavior went on for a good six months to a year, and then the grandfather arrived on the scene wanting to get involved in his treatment. Before long, the grandfather wanted to take his grandson home. By that time, the mother had just dropped away into the abyss somewhere. The grandfather had now decided that his daughter was no good and that he was going to rescue Dustin.

Dustin started acting out even more. He was difficult to control. He became "shut down" and wouldn't talk to anybody. It finally worked itself out when I decided to take another approach: I made him my best friend. I made a point to let him know that even if I didn't have any extra time to see anybody unscheduled that week, I'd still see him. I made him feel like he was the most important person in the whole unit. I stopped trying to do any routine kind of therapy in our sessions and just followed the moment.

Basically, what happened was once we met a few times without pressing into issues, he began to relax, and we just went down to the playroom to hang out. Within a short time, he began to talk about his mom. I didn't try to make his situation seem okay or minimize anything he said. I think that's really important. When the children get disconnected at that age, it's hard for them to be able to verbalize anything such as: "I miss my mother," or "I'm angry that my mother didn't stop (her boyfriend) from hitting me," or "Where is my mother? Will she ever come back?" Being able to say such things is healing. Most of the time, the children don't understand a lot about what is going on and can only specifically identify abandonment. When Dustin was able to speak out, it meant he was getting better.

The *key* is to listen. Most of the children have stopped speaking because no one *was* listening for so long. Or they were punished for speaking out. I usually just listen; I let them speak and cry if they need to. One time Dustin cried for over an hour and then fell sound asleep—exhausted. He was so full of grief that he just put his head down on the table and went out like a light.

Finally, there came the day that during one of his grandfather's visits, Dustin looked at him and demanded, "Tell me about my mom. Where is she now?"

That was a huge breakthrough because the subject of *Mom* had been a big taboo with his grandpa. You were to ask no questions about her. I refrained from saying anything but stayed poised and ready to intervene if Grandpa became inappropriate. I think Dustin could see my smile out of the corner of his eye.

"Son, you got your nose from your mom, and you got your chin from your dad, and your daddy was very handsome and very tall. You're gonna get your height from him."

"I'm gonna be tall?"

"Yes, you're gonna be really tall. Look at your feet."
And that's all the grandfather ever told Dustin about his father.

Then, he stated, "Son, your mom loves you. But she's not able to be with you right now; she has problems."

"Do you realize what progress that is?" I said to his grandpa afterward.

That meeting with his grandfather was tough, but Dustin got through it.

The inevitable moment eventually comes when you know you have to say goodbye to a child . . . and that's difficult. We have a kind of a mini-going-away party. I had some fear about letting go of Dustin. I had become very attached. I was going to miss him because he'd been with us for two years and worked so hard and come so far. He was brave and at the same time casual about the whole thing. I knew he was going to a good place but found myself worrying nonetheless. I was very protective and didn't want anything to happen to him, but I had to let go. I was torn to see him go off to his new foster home. I had come to feel as protective as a mom, sending him out into the world, unable to be there to stand up for him. That was a bittersweet day for me.

Dustin went from our facility, where he entered being almost uncontrollable, to where he was ready for a foster home. That was an enormous achievement in two years for such a young person—anyone actually. It was one of the greatest successes we'd ever had. All of us had really, really grown to love the boy.

I couldn't help but thank God the day Dustin left. His growth had been incredible—almost like a miracle right before my eyes. God really surprised me with Dustin—made me wonder . . . about a lot of things. And grateful, too.

the eagles auxiliary of childhelp usa

SOMEWHERE IN HIS MEMORY

The Eagles Auxiliary of Childhelp USA was founded 20 years ago to bring the children of the Village of Childhelp West into ongoing relationships with non-abusing, responsible adults who were neither in their school nor in therapeutic settings. It was felt that caring men and women of various ages and professions interacting with the abused children could help them move more smoothly back into the communities, if not their families.

Over the years, we have come to understand that the Eagles' experience can sometimes be about life stories that momentarily surface from deep hurt then just as quickly go below again. The Eagles Auxiliary was not created to probe or to counsel but to be present for a child undergoing a difficult healing inside—and in some cases—outside. The outward signs of abuse can often be terribly evident to the eye but rarely is the inner scar revealed. I remember a story about one child in the early years of our auxiliary.

On an excursion to Knott's Berry Farm amusement park

in California, a group of Eagles and children came upon an Old West set just as a reenactment of a shootout began. Guns firing blank bullets blazed and bodies fell to the ground—accompanied by much overacted screaming and dying. It was a theatrical Western shootout in the largest sense. However, there was something very different about a sobbing scream coming from beneath a nearby bench. This pretend shootout had suddenly become very real for a seven-year-old boy wearing a blue Eagles T-shirt. He was curled up into himself under a nearby bench, as he was reliving a real story of violence coming from somewhere in his memory.

Through his painful moans, we heard, "Daddy, Daddy! Don't shoot me!"

A mistaken entertainment? Clearly.

An opportunity? Definitely, as the first human touch to follow was not in harm, but in comfort.

In one small way, an Eagle's touch, as he reached out, helped break a connection while creating a bridge. It was an Eagle doing what the Eagles Auxiliary is supposed to do—one degree of separation was removed between child, self, and community.

That Eagle never knew the *before* and maybe very little of the *after* in the little boy's personal story. But he certainly knew what the moment called for and acted instinctively.

The Eagles Auxiliary of Childhelp West creates their own healing story each month by their presence with the children. It is that presence and connection that help each abused child begin to write a new story full of hope.

Every year, the Eagles sponsor a day of Olympic games at the Beaumont residential village. Children get to participate in creating the games—cross country running, relay races, water sports, and so forth. There is even a competition of creating the Olympics T-shirt where children can submit a design for that year. On the day of the games, each child gets a T-shirt and every participant receives at least one medal for his or her efforts. The day comes to a close with the Eagles and children sharing a meal and then on to some kite flying. It is a magnificent day put on by the Eagles for the children. Much love and laughter abound around the Village on that particular day. For all of us at Childhelp West, the Eagles truly soar!

Yvonne and Sara taking time to play.

One of the ponies donated to Childhelp USA for the children.

This is why we do what we do.

Celebrity Ambassador Pat Boone
and long time supporter Efrem Zimbalist, Jr.

Dedication ceremony of Village East, the Alice C. Tyler Village
of Childhelp East—serving children and the environment.

Sara, Alice C. Tyler, Yvonne, and Cheryl Ladd (1987).   Sara, former First Lady Barbara Bush, and Yvonne.

Play therapy at the sandbox.

Someone who's there to listen.

Ralna English, Efrem Zimbalist, Jr., Cheryl Ladd, Anne Jeffreys, and Rich Little at the Tennessee Center Fundraiser Gala (1994).

A child's "masterpiece" art.

CHAPTER FIVE

answering the call

FROM VOLUNTEERS TO ADMINISTRATORS, ONE COUPLE'S STORY OF COMMITMENT TO CHILDHELP

The first plane had just landed. None of us who had come to volunteer with Operation Babylift were prepared for what we were about to experience. The roar of the plane taxiing up to the hangar was deafening. We put our hands to our ears to soften the sound as we began to move toward this enormous aircraft. I know we all were excited that they had made it out safely and were here at last. It was such an anxious experience, watching the rear of the plane as it began to open, revealing its cargo inside. I remember thinking to myself: "Whatever you see, just keep breathing, and stay focused."

The first servicemen we could see coming out of the back of the aircraft began to beckon us to approach the entry. Sara and Yvonne signaled for us to "go." As we started up the ramp, the first sight that came into view was this ocean of children with complete fear in their eyes as they tried to understand the barrage of unknown people coming toward them. There they were, all huddled together, having no idea where they were, what was going on, or what was about to happen to them. In the center of the plane was a cache of cardboard boxes filled with babies. Yes, filled with *babies*! And in other sections, they were laid out across huge suspended canvasses and strapped down. The sound of their cries as they feared what was about to happen to them next was deafening. Most of us could not comprehend what we were seeing. Luckily, there was no time to drop into our emotions—we had to keep moving.

The children were taken to the Long Beach Naval Base. Each one of us was given a child to be responsible for until they went on to their next destination as part of this monumental adoption process. All the children who came in on that first plane were children whose paperwork had already been completed and had adoptive parents waiting for them somewhere across the globe. The little girl my husband took care of was on her way to Norway. I had a little boy headed for Canada who looked like he was a newborn, but his papers said he was six months old. This was the sad shape that most of these children were in because of the crisis that had been going on in Vietnam. To this day, I wonder how we handled it all.

That was our initial encounter with Sara, Yvonne, and what today has become Childhelp USA—a relationship that has lasted for my husband and me for nearly 30 years now.

It was at the close of the Vietnam War, and my husband Dick and I had two young children and had talked about the possibility of adopting a child. I had the television on one day, and Sara and Yvonne were on talking about the organization; at that time it was called International Orphans, Inc. They told of the project they had started with schools, hospitals, and orphanages in Japan and Vietnam. In the segment, they were sharing their story and explaining that they were going to be bringing children out of Vietnam to the United States and were looking for people who might be interested in adopting. A phone number was given for anyone who was interested.

I spoke with Dick, and we both decided this was our answer to having another child. I called immediately; gave everyone my name, Linda Willey, and number; stated that I would absolutely be interested in adopting a child—and hung up the phone after I was told someone would call me back.

I wondered, "How long will I have to wait to hear something? I want to know what's going on right now. I've made a move, now what are *they* going to do?"

After a couple days of not hearing from them, I was just jumping out of my skin.

My husband suggested, "Well, why don't you call and see if they need help at the office?"

I did. And before I knew it, I had committed both of us to showing up and helping out. Regardless of what happened about us getting to adopt, we knew we had to be involved.

It seemed like just a short time before we were notified the first planeload of children was coming into Southern California from Vietnam. What an astonishing and heart-wrenching occurrence that turned out to be, especially after the crash of the first plane of children we were trying to get out. I don't think I'll ever get over that part of the whole experience.

After the Vietnam airlift, I decided to remain involved. I was eventually asked to come onto the National Board of Directors with the organization and have remained as a volunteer for over 30 years. It was also about that time, I believe, the name of the organization changed to Childhelp USA, as the first Childhelp Village was beginning to take shape at home. Some property had been purchased for a residential treatment facility and that got everything going in the direction of the "village" concept.

I remember when we were working to get the Beaumont Village open in California. We literally opened that facility on faith. Things just kept happening so that the Village could get opened to help and treat abused children. It was one miracle after another. Many things like that have happened—and continue to happen—with this organization. I don't want to say we take miracles for granted. But we know that they're there and that they happen. And with Childhelp, they have happened day after day, year after year. Once you really get involved and committed, you know that this is God's work.

Dick has always asserted, "You know, nothing seems too extraordinary for this organization. Sometimes you can't figure out how the challenges get worked out, but they just do—every time."

As a volunteer, I used to oversee all of the different chapters that Childhelp developed. I used to travel once a month to Washington, D.C., New York, and Connecticut. On one of the trips, when I was in Washington, D.C. with my husband, just after Sara and Yvonne had opened the Village on the East Coast in Virginia, Sara called and said that a childhood sweetheart, Earl Worsham, from Knoxville, Tennessee where she had grown up had been to the opening in Virginia.

This gentleman had asked her: "Why are you doing this everywhere else, and not doing anything in your own hometown of Knoxville?"

"Of course, this is something we'd love to do," was her reply. "We haven't really ever been asked to come into the Knoxville area. Would you be willing to help?"

To that, the gentleman responded, "If I help get this started, why don't you come to Knoxville and do a Village there?"

Sara asked Dick and me if we would do some investigation and then put together a plan that we thought might be a valid approach in considering a facility in Tennessee. Dick had remained involved with Childhelp, and he and I would often travel with Sara over to Europe for meetings dealing with children's issues on an international basis. Sara was the only representative for the United States on the Board of the International Union for Child Welfare.

Dick drew out this whole plan. If Sara and Yvonne decided to go ahead with this project, then Childhelp would begin to move into a whole new spectrum of what could be done to support abused children.

After his research, Dick explained, "From what I can see, I believe there is a real need for this in the Knoxville area. If you are going to continue to grow the organization, then here's really what I believe we need to do to make an impact on the lives of these abused children."

Sara and Yvonne knew this was a huge undertaking, yet they could tell that Dick was more than enthused by the possibilities. They said they needed to review it, and "be with it" for a while. About a week later, we heard back from them with a decision.

Once they read everything Dick had put forth, they called him and said, "You know, we carefully went over all that you have laid out here, we've discussed it, talked to our National Board of Directors, and we've prayed about it. Dick, we really believe this is the way we should go. We'll start it in Tennessee. Now, would you be willing to move there and launch this? We think you would be the perfect person."

After talking with Sara and Yvonne at length, Dick asked me: "What do you want me to do?"

I responded, "I want you to do whatever it is you feel you need to do. I don't want you to be doing this just because you know how passionately I feel about this organization. It has to be something that *you* want to do, and whatever you want to do is fine with me. But it's something that must be your decision because you'll be the one who'll have to head all of this."

He thought about it, I guess, oh, for a couple days and then decided, "You know what? I really want to do it. I think this is something that I'm *supposed* to do, and I think this is something that *we* need to do. Will you go to Knoxville with me to see how we can start this?"

Of course, my answer was a resounding: "Yes!"

It was July of 1993. We had no familiarity with Knoxville *or* Tennessee. We're both native Californians. Dick had been born in Los Angeles, and I had been born in Long Beach—and we'd lived our entire lives in Southern California. Sara had grown up there and had some friends still living there. They were kind enough to show us around and introduce us to some people. After a short period of exploration, questions, and discovery, we decided this was something we could spearhead.

Dick took his retirement three months early. We packed up our house, moved by September, and started looking around to see exactly how we were going to pursue Childhelp in Knoxville, Tennessee. And that's where Childhelp's Advocacy Centers were born.

There was a really great need for an advocacy center there—a place where children were the first in priority. A center where those who had been reported as abused could be interviewed by everyone who needed to do so at once *and* in one place—the Department of Children's Services, a social worker, law enforcement, and the district attorney's office. As it was, they had been conducting these interviews separately, and then the child would be put on a waiting list for as long as six months for a forensic medical exam to see if there was any evidence of sexual abuse. By this process, it could take as long as ten months for just the interviews and tests to be concluded. Therefore, during all that time, the child was still being victimized in a different way.

When you take a very young child and put them in a situation where they're in an interrogation room time and again, they automatically begin to think something's wrong—they really *are* bad. They begin to imagine that they *must* have done something bad, otherwise they wouldn't keep bringing them back here over and over again. This is one of the things we felt we needed to do something about. We all wanted to make the process easier for the child and the family to go through. So, this is where we would start and then look at creating a Village in our later plans.

We started looking around within the community to decide where we could establish the center to handle this situation and how it would work. Dick started meeting with the Department of Children's Services and law enforcement—a familiar area for him since he had done related work in that same department while with the Los Angeles Police Department—and tried to explain to them what we were about to do and how they all would be able to use the facility.

Those meetings were going on when we received a phone call from the District Attorney of Knox County wanting to know if we could come down for a meeting.

We said, "Sure, no problem."

Well, we walked into a meeting that was filled with most every charity-sponsored organization in the city. There was one very large organization, and several flagship organizations, plus a lot of small charities within the greater Knoxville area that received money from one source. The existing charities were a bit nervous about our arrival. They were not informed of our reputation, and were in some fear that our project might drain some of their charity dollars, leaving them short.

This was a familiar scenario to us. We explained that we had been asked to come there—at least by one person—one of their city's own. We let them know that we planned to sustain the center with funds initially from the national organization of Childhelp.

"We're here, and we're committed to creating the advocacy center for these children," Dick said. "We want to work alongside you."

Well, we stayed in limbo for about three months. We didn't know where we were going to go or whether the center was going to happen. We really were just adrift.

Finally, Dick got to the point where he stated, "Well, we've got to move this along."

He went out into the surrounding counties and started talking to the Department of Children's Services in those areas.

In each surrounding county, he told them: "We would be glad to come here if you would have us, " if we weren't able to create the center in Knoxville.

Several of the other counties were thrilled. Of course, that went right back to the hierarchy in Knox County. They came to recognize that the Department of Children's Services really wanted Childhelp to stay there and finally set about helping us make this advocacy center happen.

I am amazed when I look back on it. I mean we really were the new "kid on the block," and we personally had no established credibility with people when we first arrived in the city. They knew of Sara and her family. They were an established family there. Yet there we were coming in and proposing this huge project, and they didn't even know anything about us. We had no track record with them. One thing I have learned since living here awhile now is that they had had a lot of people come through before, talk big, and just kind of move on—never doing what they said they were going to do. Ultimately, they would take us on face value and a lot of faith.

Just as we were about to move on to another county, the realtor we had been working with—who, ironically, was Sara's childhood friend and next-door neighbor—called us and said, "You're not going to believe this. But that building we looked at months ago that you thought would be perfect just fell out of contract, so it is back on the market."

Dick told her what Childhelp was prepared to offer them. After a bit of going back and forth with the owners, the bid was accepted. In two days, we went from having no idea where we were going to be launching our first program—to not only a having program—but knowing that it was going to be in Knox County. And we had the building that we knew would be the perfect place.

All this happened so quickly that we didn't have time to raise the money yet. In fact, we didn't know from where it would come. We figured we'd work all of that out.

All we had at the time from one of our National Board Members and her husband was a pledge for $100,000. Along with Sara and Yvonne, and the blessing of the National Board, we unanimously decided we must go forward—after all, by this time, we knew God was on our side. It was not about us; it was about the children.

We managed to put together a fund raising event, which turned out to be very successful. With what we had from a National Board Member and our own fundraising efforts, we had enough money to put a down payment on the building, and then have some left to begin work on the refurbishing. Once again, we were blessed by *earthly angels*. What a celebration! Knoxville would have an advocacy center after all!

It was an exciting time because everyone was working together; therefore, everyone had sweat equity invested in the build-out. It wasn't just Childhelp. It was the entire community because everyone was finally really working on making the project happen. There was no longer a feeling of people at odds over our being there. A community of people that stretched beyond the center had begun to develop.

As we continued to build out the facility, whatever we needed always seemed to show up. It was awe-inspiring how people just appeared during that time and gave so much to the "newcomers." The Childhelp center in Knoxville has turned out to be one of our most productive efforts, and we've stretched to the point of creating a mobile unit that can reach far into the surrounding rural areas. We take our services to the people; some of them have never even seen a doctor. In our first year at the center, we saw about 300 children come through. Last year, 2002, we had 544. All allegations of abuse. For the population of Knox County, that is an astounding number.

The district attorney here, who at first questioned our coming into the county, is now a huge supporter of Childhelp. He's actually on our Tennessee Board. He and his wife are strong supporters of the organization. They make monthly pledges that go toward our Village. It's wonderful. I think part of his "turnaround" resulted in the fact that we just kept doing what we were supposed to do, what we went there to do. We never said anything bad about anyone. We never criticized anyone else. We just kept doing what we knew was the next step—and what God wanted us to do. We weren't silent. We did speak out and spoke out often. We have found time after time that if we just allow ourselves to remain God-centered and focused on the heart of our mission, people will eventually understand.

My husband was at a meeting to speak, oh, probably a year after the center was built. There were about 250 people attending—prominent people in the community. The district attorney stood up and said, "You know I'm going to introduce you to someone, and I need to tell you that I wasn't for this organization when they came into this town. I did everything I could to stop it because I'd heard that this wasn't going to be a good thing. Today, I'm here to say that I was wrong. And Childhelp USA is one of the best things that has ever happened to this community."

Dick and I have been in Knoxville now for about ten years, and we have seen some wonderful things happen for the children in this community. We love what we are doing. It is making a difference. It is truly wonderful that we can work along side each other to help create a safe environment and better lives for these children who have experienced such unspeakable abuse.

From those first days during Operation Babylift until now—although that day the first plane from Vietnam landed remains vivid in my mind—we feel blessed that we have remained a part of something so important. The powerful imprint that was made on our lives walking into that plane of orphans will always hold strong. It never ceases to astonish us both what all these children have suffered. It's interesting that we initially came to this looking for a child of our own to adopt and instead ended up with many children to care for and love. When that first smile from a child who has endured such a torturous existence breaks through, when you see in their eyes that they know they are now safe, it makes whatever we have gone through to be here worthwhile. We know we are creating a space for healing. That's what Childhelp is about—creating miracles for children.

1-800-4-a-child

CHILDHELP USA'S
NATIONAL CHILD ABUSE HOTLINE

The Childhelp USA National Child Abuse Hotline serves the United States, its territories, and Canada 24 hours a day, 7 days a week. Established in 1982, the hotline is staffed by professional crisis counselors who, through translators, can provide assistance in 140 languages and to the hearing impaired. During child abuse prevention, education, and training programs, the staff hands out bookmarks to the children attending with the 800 number imprinted for them to call in case they feel they are in danger of being abused.

Childhelp USA is pleased to acknowledge the gift of $1,000,000 by well-known photographer Anne Geddes and her husband, Kel, to underwrite the hotline. More than 600 calls a day come into our National Headquarters in Arizona. With the recent visibility of the hotline increased through a nationwide Public Service Announcement campaign provided by the Ad Council Public Service Advertising which was started in June 2003, additional funding is being sought for staff and phone lines in order not to keep one child waiting "on hold" in their moment of courageous reaching out for help.

Below, we hope you get a sense of how important this support is to the abused child.

Recently, as a counselor for the Childhelp USA hotline, I had a call from a ten-year-old boy. The child informed me that he was calling from a pay phone in front of a convenience store. He was crying. He nervously asked if the call was being taped and whether his mother and stepfather would find out about it. I assured him that the call was anonymous. He had been given a bookmark at his school that tells children about Childhelp's hotline and when they should call for help.

Through his tears, the child asked me if I believed in angels. Since the focus of each call is the caller, I asked the boy if *he* believed in them. He replied that he had been very close to his grandmother who died last year, and she had told him that he should ask his guardian angel for help when in trouble. She said God created the angels to help us.

The boy went on to say he was very unhappy since his parents got a divorce and his mother remarried. His real father is with the Air Force and stationed in England. He had not seen him in two years.

After much assurance that I was there to listen and to help, the boy told his story. It seems he looks a lot like his dad. Whenever his mother was angry with him, she hit him with a belt on his arms and legs and told him she hated him because he was just like his father. She often hit him with the belt buckle, which left marks that bled. It seemed mom was always angry with him, and he felt lots of times for no reason. He was beaten for smiling, or not answering quickly enough, or for not putting his toothbrush back in the cabinet just so. He never knew *when* she was going to hit him.

When asked if he could talk to his stepdad about it, he adamantly said "no" because he felt the stepfather hated him because he wasn't his son. His stepdad pretty much ignored him and only spent time with the new eight-month-old baby.

When asked if there was a teacher or counselor at school to talk to he replied, "Oh no, my mother said she would take me out of town in the car and leave me in the middle of nowhere if I told."

His mother had just beaten him before calling the hotline. She pulled out some of his hair and burned the top of one hand with the iron. I asked what had caused her to do this. His answer was she found a dirty sock on the floor of his closet. The child stated to his mom that he didn't want to live and ran out of the house planning to jump in front of a big truck. He told me he wanted to die and be in heaven with his grandmother.

He then told me that just as he was running for the freeway to look for an oncoming truck, he stuck his hand in his pocket and discovered the rumpled bookmark with the hotline number on it. He stopped and looked up to see a phone booth in front of the nearby convenience store. He decided he would take the risk and call.

The story went on as I conferenced him in on a call to both the police and Child Protective Services. We have the ability to do that from the hotline headquarters. I stayed on the line and helped him make the report and continued to stay on the line until the child was on his way to a safe place.

The child's last words to me were, "I knew my grandma was right. There are angels, and today you were mine."

It's calls like this that make us proud of what we do on the hotline at Childhelp USA.

watch for me!

YOU'RE NEVER TOO YOUNG TO MAKE A DIFFERENCE

*P*eter sat down and motioned for me to come closer, and then he told me that he loved me. He whispered it, as if he were somewhat ashamed, and then abruptly said, "Thank you." He put his arms around me, and we hugged for what seemed an eternity. Even though I was young myself at the time, something inside me could feel his pain. I wanted to wrap my arms around this young boy and protect him from all evil—and never let anyone ever hurt him again.

Peter lived at one of the villages of Childhelp where he had been sent for help because of his severe abuse. This innocent child's parents were in jail for sexually and physically abusing him at the age of six, and he had been at the Village for five years. He was progressively getting better.

Unlike Peter, I am a 17-year-old girl who has grown up in a secure home, where abuse and poverty are nowhere to be found. My best friend is my mother, and my parents are happily married. I cannot imagine growing up without my family's love and support. My family is my world. They have taught me that everyone I meet can have an impact on my life and that I can help make a positive impact on others' lives.

At the age of six, I was chasing butterflies and playing tea party with my mom and all of my close friends. When Peter turned six, he was separated from his family and friends and sent to the Childhelp Village to live with a group of young boys with similar challenges. There were doctors there who would try to help. I cannot imagine my childhood without birthday parties dressed as a princess or without weekly family monopoly game nights.

When I met Peter, I was only ten and did not understand the differences between him and me. My mother and father had briefly explained to me that we were going to visit the Village and play with some children who were very lonely. At first, I didn't want to make new friends because I liked the ones I already had; however, my parents finally convinced me to go. I was too naïve and sheltered to have been told at that time the truth at such a young age. I wouldn't have fully understood the seriousness of Peter's situation.

Peter was a boy with whom I ended up spending five years—laughing, holding hands, and simply learning to love. I tried to instill in his heart and soul that he is a person who deserves to be loved and that he should have dreams and goals. During that time, he decided he wanted to be one of the best soccer players in the world.

When he first arrived at the Village, Peter was like a wounded bird, dependent on everyone for the simplest things. When he was ready to leave, he was still unsure about certain things but confident that he was going to succeed. Peter called me the day that he was leaving to tell me that he wouldn't get to see me anymore. He was crying. He said he would miss me. I knew I had succeeded in making a difference in his life when, toward the end of the conversation, the tone in his voice suddenly changed and he proudly told me to look for him playing soccer in the World Cup in a few years. I was so excited that he was living his dream.

Because of my experience with Peter, I want to dedicate much of my life to Childhelp. There is nothing more fulfilling than to see a child's face brighten up simply because of something I might have done. These children who have had such heartbreaking early lives have the chance to be a vital part of our society if they receive the necessary love and support. They can grow into productive, positive human beings. This is what Childhelp does, and I want to be an ongoing part of that.

Peter went from having his self-esteem at a record low to having the confidence in himself that he would someday be a famous soccer player. It took five years of practicing soccer, counseling, and unconditional love to get him to where he is today. He is not completely healed, but his scars are mending. Peter showed perseverance and determination far more than any young person I have ever met. While I feel fortunate that I never had to go through something as traumatic as that in my life, I also feel proud to think that I helped soften someone's pain—that someone has more confidence in himself or herself, I believe, is because I stuck by his or her side.

Every time I see a child or infant, I find myself gazing into his or her eyes and praying that he or she is being raised in a loving family. Every night before my dreams take over and I am swept away from reality, I take a moment to hope and wish that all sheltered people, like myself, may be touched by someone as special as Peter. The kind of social life I have, the size of my bank account, or the clothes I am wearing will not matter 20 years from now. What will be important—as it is now—is that I am making a difference in the life of a child. I realize that life is about making a difference and letting people know you care. We're all programmed to measure our value by the material things we possess; yet some of the most important things in life are developing the relationships where we can make a difference. I am grateful to my parents for connecting me to Childhelp, for my loving home, and for what I have learned going to the Village and being with Peter.

A time for peaceful thinking.

The spirit of Childhelp USA.   Art is healing.

Dionne Fedderson Archer (Yvonne's daughter), John Hopkins (Sara's son), Lynne Cheney, and Sylvia Hopkins (John's wife) at the Humanitarian Awards Luncheon (2003).

CHAPTER SIX

the spirit
of childhelp

A VILLAGE CHAPLAIN TALKS
ABOUT NURTURING THE SOUL

Recently, a six-year-old boy asked me: "How does God speak to you, Chapelman?"

Having affectionately grown accustomed to the nickname the children at the Village had given to me, I answered the young boy by saying God usually spoke to me in prayer.

"Okay, let's try that," the boy blurted out.

"Right now?" I asked.

"Sure," the boy replied.

He then went on to instruct me that we would have to be absolutely quiet to pray. The two of us sat in perfect silence for about three minutes—an extraordinarily long time for a six-year-old child.

Then the boy inquired, "Did you hear him yet?"

I had to admit that I hadn't heard God speaking to me during that particular prayer. The boy was astonished.

"Well, I heard him," he stated in a matter-of-fact way.

I then asked what God had said to him.

"God told me He loves all of the children of the Village

and He wants them to be safe," the boy said, looking me in the eyes. Tears welled up, and my heart felt a huge tug.

Reflecting upon the incident later in the day, I realized that God had, indeed, spoken to me—through the voice of a child.

At the Childhelp USA Villages, the children participate in an interfaith spiritual program. Sara and Yvonne, our founders, have made it a priority and is one of many programs that help restore the children to health. I came to the Childhelp Village as a chaplain because I wanted these children to begin to understand right away that there's a difference between who we are as a person and the things we do. I wanted to be part of a team that uses spirituality as a tool for healing, and I also wanted to be part of the team that was creating those tools. With those in mind, I have done study in most every faith so that I can honor the personal aspects in each child's faith—if they have one. "The Ladies," Sara and Yvonne, take great pride in our spiritual programs. They have a strong belief that it was God who brought them to do this work in the first place.

They have said many times: "God never abandoned us, and we have no intention of abandoning Him."

As a chaplain, this is the environment I work in everyday. The concept of using spirituality as a tool for healing has been a keen interest of mine for many years. I knew the idea was already being explored with teenagers and the older; I wanted to see that same set of tools work in some way for children. These children. The ones who come to us come as empty vessels for the most part. There is not very much hope left in their little lives. That is something that touches me deeply, and I want to do whatever I can to re-ignite that spark of hope.

As young children, most are taught to believe that God loves things that are good, and God hates things that are bad. Therefore, it's not too far of a theological stretch for them to believe that "God doesn't like me because I am bad." I mean they may not say that verbally; they may not be able to articulate that in word form. But I think subconsciously they really, truly believe it. If you were to ask most of these children who come here: "Who created the world?" The answer you would receive is usually: "Well, God created it." I don't know how you start to do therapy with a child who believes that God created everything that is going on around him or her, but God doesn't like them. That's like a big, cosmic angst hanging over their heads that you're just not going to be able to get rid of very easily. Yet I am passionate about doing something about it. Many times I have looked deeply into the sadness, loss, and hurt that lie behind the eyes of these children. It has taken my breath away at what I have seen—and have heard.

What we try to incorporate in their healing, as a part of the spiritual program we provide at a Village, is a starting place to help them understand that how they have been treated up to now is not because they were bad. It's the people around them before they came who did things that weren't good. They're *not* the problem. We try to explain to the child that neither did they ask for what happened nor did they deserve it. And certainly God loves them. God is not mad at them for anything that has happened. And I always talk to children about the fact that God loves us all unconditionally.

When a child first arrives, all the major players of the team who will be interacting with the child sit down together to create a "Master Treatment Plan" for the first 60 days. We give ourselves a bit of time to observe the child so that we can present our evaluation from the point of view of our individual expertise. This is exciting because you really get the time to create an in-depth overview of the child—a holographic image—that is not some one-dimensional assessment coming off a piece of paper. Within those 60 days, we are able to get a pretty good idea of the behavioral patterns, their health needs, and their educational and literacy backgrounds. Everyone respects the other's expertise, and it all comes together quite well. I think what we do here as a team to evaluate the child is unique—sometimes quite cutting-edge—in that we *really* take the time to understand each child. We have a chance for some degree of flexibility in our approach during the observations governed by the individuality of each child. They are just not one more "number" once again. It allows us to bring to the table information that is so much more thorough.

We have a chapel on the grounds, and we have two "services" on Sunday mornings. Our approach to what we call "service" runs outside the borders of what most think of as certainly a mainstream Sunday service. We take a non-denominational approach. It is all geared to the children: boosting their self-esteem and trust. It's about feeding the soul. Children's Bibles are made available for each child, and we create new stories based from the stories found in there that are then connected to a larger story that usually involves some principle for living. What we try to do is get the principle or some other tool for living across to them. And they get to help with the stories. Many times, I have seen that when a child has been participating in creating a story, his or her own story begins to come out. It is easier for the "secret" that has been kept in silence to break through under the guise of a character who is not them. When dealing with crises in their life, most people end up connecting it to a larger story to be able to move through its impact. It is like opening the valve on a pressure cooker. You can almost hear an audible sigh of relief that the "secret" has been released. And yet the child is not rendered vulnerable because "the character said it," not them.

Afterward I'll talk to them about the story. I'll try to tie it in together with a character pillar we're working on that month. Part of that character pillar is designed in some way to help the children work through a whole particular issue. They take the stories and relate to them. There are many stories that can be used to portray dysfunctional families with unhealthy behaviors to use. I want to give them a sense of *who* they really are. I want them to know that what has happened to them happened also to other people. And it's been happening for years and centuries. I also want them to see the options they might have in any given situation. I want them to learn to trust that somewhere, somehow, someone or something will help them through the rough times. Never, never give up hope; the miracle is just around the corner.

Coming to the chapel also gives the children a beginning sense of what a supportive atmosphere can be like. I want to create a situation where they feel like they fit in. There are also several opportunities for participation during Sunday mornings on different levels. One child is appointed as a "chapel helper." I go to the cottage and pick him or her up about a half-hour before chapel starts. We go down to the chapel and begin to set things up. When the children participate in the service, they get to experience the feeling of what it is like to be part of something, not just a spectator.

There are very few people in the United States, and this is one of the first to my knowledge, doing this process of using spirituality with children for healing. When I talk to the few others I know, we always sort of kid that we could hold our nationwide convention in a closet somewhere because there simply aren't that many people who are doing this sort of approach to healing. I am proud to be a part of it.

One of the tools we use in chapel is a karaoke machine. What it basically does is it gives the presence of something powerful. The children here gravitate toward power. Power is something that makes them feel safe. In their experience, whoever was in the house who had the most power was the person who was the safest. So, using the karaoke machine gives them a "power fix" when they're using the microphone, and they're learning to use power in a positive way instead of a negative way. I want to encourage them to do that.

The two ways they get to use the microphone in chapel are by giving the news and reading the prayer. There are a lot of things about reading in public that builds up one's self-confidence. When they reach those higher levels, you then encourage them by reading in public to the rest of the children who are there. The news is basically like announcements—which cottage I'm having dinner with Wednesday night (I do this each week), who's new to the Village, who has moved from one cottage to the other, children who've left the Village, and those who have birthdays coming up in the next week. The prayer is one that I've written out, and one child gets to read it while all the rest of the children in turn repeat it phrase by phrase. This promotes learning how to be a positive leader. Twice as many children sign up to do the prayer as to do the news. It is a great self-esteem builder. Then what we do is to have one child who has been selected from each cottage come up and lead a song that I pre-recorded just for them to sing along with. Quite often, this is when the child's personality starts to leak through. What a joy this is to watch!

Chapel here in the Village serves as another place in their "new life" where they know they can go for a sense of community and safety. It represents a place they can go to connect with people. It's part of Sara and Yvonne's policy that each child gets a set of chapel clothes each Christmas and Easter, along with the regular new clothes they need. Coming to chapel on Sunday is a time when they can dress up in a distinctive way. It is amazing to see how they change when they wear these clothes. They feel different about themselves. They carry themselves differently. Some have never had clothes that were special and were only theirs for "occasions." One child will actually be the one who gets to ring the chapel bell to call the others to service. The children love that assignment.

Finally, one of my most favorite things we have created is called "Sharing Time." I love this because of what happens as the outcome. Each child in the Village receives an average of $3.00 to $5.00 a month allowance—older children get more, younger children get less. What we do is have them bring with them pennies, nickels, dimes, and quarters. Then someone will take this plate and actually pass it around to all the children in the chapel. When both services are over, I have a chapel helper who helps me count up the money. We then find a homeless shelter or some other place with children and ask them what they might need in the way of supplies for their children—construction paper, watercolors, tempera paint, and oftentimes food. When we have the sum of $25.00, we take a group of children to the store and buy these things with the money saved and deliver them to the designated place. The children learn to discern what to buy for the money so that whatever they do purchase can benefit the other children the most. This also helps our children learn about making decisions.

When children arrive, they do so pretty much with just the clothes on their back. Whatever "stuff" they have is usually in a trash bag. They feel very disposable. On the average, this is their fifth or sixth placement by the time they get here. That boils down to a lot of negative kind of failure implanted in their minds. I want to let the children know that they can feel good about who they are by helping *other* people. And, frankly, most of the children who come here do not feel powerful enough to be able to help anyone else. That's why the sharing trip is terribly important in a number of different ways.

One of the first things it does is to help them learn that "I can help somebody else." The second thing is that when we go to the store, we have a list, and we follow the list, and we don't purchase things for ourselves. They've rarely had to have that focus in buying before. Most of the time, they never went to the store with any list at all. It was just impulse buying and shopping for whatever money they had to spend. They usually learned to keep silent when and if one of them had any extra money at all, or it would be taken away. The third thing is it teaches a sense of self-discipline: I have a list, this is the project, and I'm going to the store to purchase these things *only*. Then I am going to deliver it to the place we have designated.

The fourth lesson is empathy.

When we start off the trip, what I say to the children going is, "Now, when you need to go shopping there are gonna be 155,000 different things you're gonna want, because they're all placed at your level when you go to check out, okay? But this trip isn't for us. It's for . . ."

They invariably finish off that sentence by always responding, "The poor children."

As we are returning in the van, I usually say, "Would the children at the mission have gotten construction paper, tempera paint, and water colors if you had not been there today?"

And they say, "No."

To which I reply, "Well, you made a difference in their lives, didn't you, by being there today?" If that doesn't do something for your soul, I don't know what will. Such beautiful children they really are inside. There is that place of innocence and tenderness harbored somewhere deep within.

I remember a child I met on one of my Wednesday dinners at the cottages. His name is Charlie. He was having a hard time with his schoolwork. I made a deal with him that if he brought his grades up to a certain point, the two of us would go out to dinner somewhere. The children just love having individual time where they get to go wherever they want to and pick whatever they want to do. Charlie did bring his grades up, and we made a plan to go out and have dinner. Of course, he wanted to go to McDonald's. So, we ate dinner at McDonald's.

He looked over and asked, "Can we have dessert?"

I thought, "Well, this is not a real expensive menu here at McDonald's. Yeah, I don't think we'll have any problem with dessert." So, I answered, "Sure, what do you want for dessert?"

"Donuts!" he replied. "Well, they don't have donuts here."

And he said, "No, but the donut store is like two doors down."

I agreed, "Okay, we can go get donuts."

We left McDonald's. We were walking down the sidewalk, and I saw this homeless gentleman lying on the grass as we were walking between the two places. He began to speak with us, so we just kind of keep cruising on and going down to the donut store.

When we started back, the same gentleman was there and asked me: "Can I have some money for some food?"

I answered, "No, thank you, not today."

Then Charlie asked him: "Are you hungry?"

And the guy responded, "Yeah."

Charlie reached into his bag, pulled out a couple donut holes, and gave them to him.

The guy said, "Thank you."

Once we were on our way back to the Village, Charlie turned to me and asked, "How come you didn't like helping that guy? I like helping people who are hungry."

I replied, "I like helping people who are hungry, too. But he didn't ask me for food; he asked me for money."

Charlie said, "Yeah?"

I inquired, "Well, why do you suppose he's out on the streets?"

And Charlie responded, "Because he didn't get a high school education?"

"Well, that may have something to do with it. I would think that maybe something—and this is just my suspicion— I think he might be on the streets because maybe he's connected in some way with alcohol or some sort of drug abuse. If I gave him money, he might use it for those things."

Charlie replied, "Oh, okay."

I said, "What you did was absolutely right. You gave him food, and that was the right thing to do."

He sat there for a while, and then he stated, "Drugs aren't that expensive. My mom used to buy them all the time."

I answered, "Oh?"

Then he remarked, "The judge told her that she had to decide between her children and drugs."

And then there was deafening silence.

It was pretty clear what she had chosen. After what seemed like an eternity, I knew I must speak. I couldn't just leave it at this.

And so I stated, "You know she made a bad choice, because I don't know any drug in the world that's worth more than you are. I can't imagine what that'd be."

Charlie just looked over and said, "Really?"

I so wished those words had come from the person he really needed to hear it from.

Christmas is an extraordinary time at the villages. There is a party given for the children, and each child here at the Village gets paired with his or her Special Friend. If someone doesn't have his or her Special Friend that day for some reason, we attempt to find a replacement. My wife and family are usually there—my wife teaches second grade, so she's really into children. We make it known that if some child doesn't have a pairing, we are happy to be that for them. As it turned out this one Christmas, there was this one boy, D.K., whose Special Friend was unable to attend. We joyfully stepped in, and he went around with us that day. I remember he was just so polite.

He would talk on and on with my son, Jason, who was about 17. He had come to know Jason by him coming to the Village with me at times.

D.K. would ask me later: "How's Jason doing? How's things going for Jason?" Things like that.

In terms of his background and history, I know that he was on the streets at age five—basically abandoned. There were several months when he was in South Central L.A. just living off people from door to door because his mother was never around. You would think if you were in that kind of environment that you'd learn to get hard really fast. You know what I mean? That you wouldn't attach to people, you'd learn not to trust people. But D.K. was just resilient— I guess—is the best way to put it. He's in junior high school, getting straight A's, and his Childhelp foster family is talking about adopting him. It's just an absolutely, incredibly, positive story. I mean things like that give me the faith to keep going.

I distinctly recall talking to him about his time in the streets—about whether he was ever afraid and lonely. He told me that, yes, sometimes he was pretty scared.

I asked, "What'd you do?"

And he stated, "Well, I just usually hid behind a fence or under something."

Can you imagine a child of this age on the streets alone? Incomprehensible!

I queried, "Well, if you ever got in a situation like that again, what would you do now?"

He responded, "I guess I'd just pray about it first."

I thought that kind of shows some of his development in a spiritual way. Then, he did not feel like he was alone or that he didn't have somebody—whereas before he came here, he definitely felt he left out and nobody was around.

I guess the thing that really makes me feel good is to see that he has actually gotten connected with a family who loves him and that he's not out there wandering around. He's actually with people who are caring and concerned for him.

What we do here in our spiritual program has great potential for healing. I see it time and again. It may sound simple, what we do, yet the results are gratifying. It helps create a sense of hope, trust, and safety. I try not to get too emotionally attached because of the work that we're doing here. But like anything else you care deeply about, sometimes it's a challenge. The fact is that we are not the end-stop. The end-stop is to get each child to a family, so then they can be with people who are going to love and care for them on an ongoing basis. Forever and ever, amen. That's the main stop. We're like this way-station that helps them get there. Sometimes that's hard to do, you know. It's hard to keep being purposeful about that, I guess, is the best way for me to put it. Because you know what? There's a girl who left last week, and there's a young girl coming in today who needs to be here just as much as the girl who just left. There's always another child out there who's ready to come here. There's always another child who needs our attention, and one who needs a miracle in his or her life. I live each day believing that there is something we can do to help begin the healing once the silence is broken.

I've been privileged to see the miracles time and time again. They never stop!

god made a mistake

OUR CHALLENGE
TO REWRITE NEGATIVE INPUT

*I*t was Sunday afternoon. A group of boys and I were sitting around talking. I am one of the chaplains at a Village. I had stayed after the Sunday service to spend some time with them. The boys were having a great time bouncing from one topic of discussion to another.

One of the boys began recounting an event that had occurred earlier in the week. Then another boy who felt the need to correct some errors in the story being told quickly interrupted him.

"No, it didn't happen three times. It happened four!"

The boy who had been telling the story replied, "I made a mistake. Big deal!"

An argument ensued because the second boy was not willing to drop the issue. He wanted to argue.

I decided to help resolve the argument and interjected, "I bet we've all made mistakes. I know I have. I don't really know anyone who hasn't made a mistake."

Another of the boys said, "God doesn't make mistakes. He is perfect."

It was quiet for a moment as everyone contemplated the boy's statement, then looked at me, and waited for my response. Just as I started to say something, out of the silence came the small but determined voice of ten-year-old Sammy—one of the boys in the group.

"God *does* make mistakes. God made a mistake when He made *me*."

Well, the other boys and myself could feel the weight of Sammy's statement.

After a long pause, one of the boys responded, "Yeah, sometimes we all think that about ourselves because that's how it looks. When no one wants you, you might think you are a mistake. But I still think God doesn't make mistakes."

I know that each child is a beautiful creation of God. But you can see from this story what happens in the mind of a child who has suffered abuse. Because of the abuse Sammy experienced, he began believing a lie. The lie goes something like this: "I must deserve to be hurt; I must be bad. God must have made a mistake in making me."

Tragically, many children who have been abused blame themselves. By nature, a young child places his or her parents on a pedestal. It seems reasonable then that if they are being "punished," it must be because they deserve it. It is my passion to see that these children come to learn that they are worthwhile—that they are indeed beautiful creations. With loving support and safekeeping, we all can begin to help them rewrite their story from one of hopelessness to one of possibilities.

listen to your heart

TRUSTING THE VOICE WITHIN

During one of the Sunday Chapel Services, I told the children a Bible story about a king and his son, Jonathan. "When the king was unhappy," I told them, "he called in a boy named David who would play his harp to comfort the king. Over the years, David and the king's son, Jonathan, became the best of friends. Then, one day, Jonathan overheard his father plotting to kill David. Jonathan was faced with a serious decision. Should he be a faithful son and conceal his father's plot, or should he be a good friend and warn David?"

I asked the children what they thought. Quickly, their hands shot up into the air. All agreed that Jonathan should warn his friend. They said they felt that no one should be silent when someone was about to do something that would cause another harm.

Then one little boy spoke up and stated, "When my father was trying to kill my mother, I went to a neighbor for help."

Another child then spoke saying that when her mother's boyfriend was molesting her, she broke the silence, and told her teacher. The stories continued and I noticed how many of these children had been forced to make adult decisions in their abusive worlds. For them, crises had become ordinary.

Most of the children we get at Childhelp have lived in such abusive situations that it is no question as to why they become problematic and act out. It is the only release they have. One child I remember had had "bad boy" burned into his back by cigarettes. When we get these children, it is an uphill journey all the way to build any amount of trust with them and to get them to believe someone cares. This is probably the first time they have been in an atmosphere where they have someone to listen to them and where they are not judged for their behavior.

Finally, at the end of this Sunday story time, a small boy raised his hand.

"You just have to listen to your heart, no matter what," he told the other children, "cause somewhere inside of us, where we feel our feelings, like in our hearts, there's a little voice. Not really a voice that talks out loud. But if you really listen, you can hear it. And it will know what you should do."

That did it for me. I realized what we are doing here works. There is a place of innocence still left in these children just waiting to speak out once again—no matter how much someone has tried to silence it. Their wisdom belies their young years.

well, then, i don't belong here

A YOUNG GIRL'S STORY OF FAITH

We had never seen any child want to have a real home and be adopted more than little Alisa. Her conversation inevitably came back to: "One day, I'm going to have a mommy and daddy who love me. I may even have a dog, but I'll definitely have a mommy and daddy—a family."

At seven years old, she was almost a model child. She would sit like a little lady, say "please and thank you" when other children her age would forget. She wanted to learn things to do in the cottages. She wanted her bed to be made the best. She asked to learn to fold laundry because, she said, "I want to help my mommy when I have one."

Alisa had eventually been given away by her father, and her mother was nowhere to be found. The father had been physically abusive, and she had been sexually abused by her foster parents. Her father had constantly put her down and reprimanded her if she did not have everything in place. He forced her into the mother role in more ways than one. Therefore, Alisa's message in those early years was that if she could be the perfect image her father continually badgered her about, she'd be accepted. Her pattern developed that if she worked continuously to please everyone and do everything for him or her, she would be loved.

This would be part of our challenge in redirecting Alisa's perceptions of what was expected of her. She was only seven years old. Her eyes were soft and warm, denoting an inside tenderness that would melt your heart. Her natural curls bounced as she walked. She proved to be an extremely bright child and had a great fascination for spiritual things.

We came to realize that one of the greatest comforts for Alisa after settling into the Village was being around the chapel and the chaplain. She had a visible peace about her when she was in the chapel at the Village. She wanted to help prepare for Sunday Services, and she loved biblical stories.

One day, she stated to the chaplain: "God sometimes is the only one who listens to me—for you see, He loves me."

Alisa was quite positive she would one day be "selected" for a home and family. She kept saying to the staff: "Have you found anyone who wants me yet?" She kept inquiring what she could do to make a family want to adopt her. She would behave perfectly around any visitor or Childhelp member at the Village functions. Everyone commented what an extremely polite child she was, how well mannered. They could see she was unusual in her desire to make them feel comfortable. She would inquire about their family, asking if they had children.

One day, a family came to see the Village with friends who had supported Childhelp for many years. Alisa displayed her charm and this family was indeed captivated. They expressed surprise at such maturity in a child of her age. Alisa asked them—as she had done so many times to nearly everyone she had met—"Do you have children?" They said no, and she retorted, "Would you like one?" They replied, "We like children—maybe one day." "Would you like me?" she quickly questioned.

They were so taken by her, and the couple inquired about her background and availability. The staff and social worker allowed them to visit Alisa often, and they seemed to enjoy their weekly visits. It was finally agreed that Alisa could have a sleep-over weekend with them, with the idea in mind of indeed adopting this lovely child. Alisa was ecstatic. She knew they were interested in adopting her.

She carefully packed her clothes and told the staff and other children in her cottage: "If I'm really good and do everything perfect, I'll be adopted. I just know it. I'm going to do everything to help. And guess what? I won't only have a family, but a dog, too. They have a dog named Brownie, and I'll hug him and love him and tell him I've come to take care of him, too."

Never was a little girl so breathlessly happy at the prospect of a home—her home—at last.

When she left with the couple, her eyes literally danced and her walk was a skip.

When Alisa arrived at the couple's home, she played with the dog and met two children who lived across the street. She helped remove the dishes from the table and eagerly asked what more she could do. The wife suggested they go unpack her clothes.

As Alisa handed each piece to her to hang up, the wife commented, "Oh, what a pretty dress!"

Alisa quickly answered, "Yes, these are my chapel clothes. I'll wear them to go to church tomorrow."

To this, Alisa heard the reply, "Oh, we don't do that around here."

Alisa was shocked and inquired, "Never?"

"No, never," was the response.

Alisa looked down, tears welling up, and regretfully said,

"Well, then, I guess I don't belong here after all."

Upon returning to the Village on Sunday afternoon, Alisa sadly related the story to the cottage caregiver. Upon hearing this, the staff was astonished she'd forfeit the chance that she had longed for most of her life.

When they asked Alisa why she'd pass up this opportunity that she'd so wanted, she replied, "I know I don't belong. I know it right in here." And she pointed to her heart.

Although Alisa was disappointed beyond belief, there was an inner "knowingness" about her that seemed to sustain her. She never questioned her decision once.

There is a happy fairytale ending to Alisa's story, though.

The chaplain told this story at a ministers' convention shortly after. A pastor and his wife, a childless couple, stepped forward and announced that they would like to meet Alisa. Within four months after meeting her, they fell in love with her and adopted her. You could almost see Alisa's heart smile.

Oh, yes—and they had two dogs.

From chaos

to peace.

CHAPTER SEVEN

beyond band-aids

CARING TOLD FROM THE VIEW OF A HEALTH CARE PROVIDER

I never will forget the horror that flooded me the time I began the examination of a new little girl who had entered the Village. As the nurse assisting me unbuttoned the child's blouse, beneath, we were to reveal scar tissue that was in the imprint of an iron on this darling girl's chest. Her eyes were cast down toward the floor in embarrassment, and I was instantly grateful she wasn't looking at me to see the flash of astonishment that I am sure was registering on my face. She was only seven at the time. As we continued, another was to be found on her side.

"That must have hurt, huh?" was all I could think of to say at the moment as I tried to swallow the huge lump that was expanding in my throat.

"Yes," she answered. "I knocked over my soda when my momma was ironing."

God, hold me steady. I thought to myself.

She spoke as if she thought she had deserved it—this had been her conditioning. How could anyone do something like this? How could anyone have so little regard for human life—for helpless children?

We would later send her to have cosmetic surgery, but the remnants of the scarring would always remain as a constant reminder—a source of embarrassment. This beautiful child would grow up having to think selectively about everything she chose to wear for fear that her "nightmare" would be exposed. It created her shame. I believe that by just showing that we cared and loved her, no matter what, some of the emotionally buried pain was put to ease.

I can't begin to tell you what has come through the doors of the medical office over the many years I have been here at Childhelp. Astounding. It goes way beyond Band-Aids and medications. I am the Director of Nursing. As the nurse practitioner here at one of the Villages, it is my responsibility to coordinate the care of the children, including psychiatric care, and their general physical health care. I do all their physicals on admission and all their acute care once a year. If the children become sick or injured, I'm their first stop. I'm pretty much on call 24/7.

I am so grateful that we have an extraordinary staff of professionals here to address all aspects of the abuse these children have been exposed to in their young lives. The ripple effect on the children who have suffered is far reaching. Child abuse, so often, is the "silent killer." Until Sara and Yvonne started all this, no one was talking about this epidemic in this country. They broke the silence and continue to bring a voice to this injustice. I am proud to be a part of it.

We had one little boy who had this tattoo pinpointed on his hand with a pencil by his father for identity. He had done this to all his children.

I found this out as I was examining him one day and asked, "How'd you get that? Did somebody stab you with a pencil?"

He replied, "No, my dad put that there. He told us children he put that there so he could keep track of who we are."

"You mean he tattooed your brothers and sisters, too?"

"Uh-huh. He had a hard time remembering who we were."

The boy's dad was a schizophrenic and one night had done this to his children in a fit of anger because he was having a hard time coping with their identities.

I was thinking, "Oh, my gosh. This child has this tattoo stabbed into his hand, and the memory of it happening implanted in his mind." Every time he looks at his hand and he sees that, it reminds him of his father who was totally bonkers. For a lot of these children, something like that can also send a message that their bodies are disposable. It can lead to bouts of self-mutilation or inflicting other kinds of bodily injury to themselves. We can use laser surgery to correct the hand, yet erasing the tattoo in this child's memory is not so easy. And a lot of these children have been accustomed to the unhealthy atmosphere created in their homes that they don't even realize they have the right to be angry about what has happened to them. Working with the therapeutic staff here is the first time they have ever been allowed to show any anger. Even more heartbreaking is that most don't know there is any other way to live than what they have been exposed to in these abusive homes.

We never know when a child will have a breakthrough and start expressing anger. Sometimes that can erupt like a volcano at a moment's notice. That is why I am on call 24 hours 7 days a week. I think that on the worst weekend I've had, I was paged 19 times from Friday evening to Monday morning. And most of them were valid concerns or emergencies. Needless to say, I didn't get much rest that weekend.

I like to get to know the children. I know every single one of them, and I can tell you any of their names. You just form a real bond with these children right away. You read their history. And you might think that it's all a blur, but it's not. I know whose father killed the mother in front of them; I know all the scenarios the children have experienced. I'm really personally involved with all the boys and girls. I couldn't do it any other way.

I visit the cottages everyday so that the children become familiar with my presence. I want them to know that they can come to me anytime that they have some health issue. Many have come with much more to share. I like to see, first hand, how the children are doing. The children know I come around, and sometimes one will run up to me and say he or she needs to see me. Often there is something they want to tell me that they are uncomfortable revealing to some other staff member, especially something they're embarrassed about. So it's important, I feel, that they know I will be coming by, and that they can approach me.

Each staff member knows that if a child complains of not feeling well, it's not the child care worker's responsibility to make a decision about whether the child is truly sick, or whether he or she is using manipulative behavior, and doesn't want to go to school. If a child complains that he or she doesn't feel well, the childcare worker's responsibility is to bring that child to the medical department, and let us make that decision.

Sometimes it is a matter of the child making his or her illness up because he or she has a problem in school. That's an issue that needs to be addressed by another staff member. By not ignoring the child and allowing him or her to come to see me, we usually know quite rapidly if something is actually physically wrong with the child. The main thing we want to get across is that when the child speaks, he or she is acknowledged and not discounted or brushed away. They've seen enough of that. We open the clinic office at 7:30 every morning. On some mornings, we will see 20 children before school time.

We know a lot about each child's history before he or she even arrives at a village. There is a huge amount of paper work that goes back and forth prior to their arrival, but there are always surprises that begin to slip out once the child realizes they are in a safe environment.

One of those surprises came with a little boy who was about seven when he came here. He had been so neglected that he had become totally withdrawn and rarely spoke. He seemed to be in good health, yet the staff kept telling me they felt something was wrong because he constantly seemed to have difficulty eating and swallowing. He had said that it hurt to swallow.

Upon a routine examination, nothing appeared to be inflamed. The staff would not let up that there was something wrong, so I decided to take him for a more thorough examination off grounds. To my horror, what was found was that a quarter was lodged deep down in his throat. It was removed successfully, and it was guessed that it might have been there for about four years. Can you imagine? He would have been about three and had probably forgotten the incident itself, only mindful of the constant discomfort, and not remembering why it might be occurring. I am grateful we have such a wonderful staff that kept speaking out about this child until we uncovered the problem. No wonder he rarely spoke. It must have been painful to even try.

There was rarely silence in his presence after that. He chattered away day and night, and his personality blossomed.

When he left here, he was a child with self-esteem and quite a handsome young man who was doing well in school.

I have a passion for this work and these children. I am totally invested in their healing. I had a very happy childhood. Ever since I can remember, as a young child, I just thought that children deserved to be heard and loved. But I was just always really tuned into that. I've always been a very sensitive person, and I've felt sorry for children—like some friends of mine—who didn't have a good solid family. When I started nursing, I was working as a newborn intensive care nurse for the Army. And now I am here. I would have never guessed this is where I would end up.

Once when I was visiting my mother, she went up into the attic and came back with this drawing I had done when I was seven years old. It was a drawing of a hospital, and I had written on that drawing: "When I grow up I want to be a nurse who helps children and their families." I had completely forgotten about that. I had it framed and is on my wall. I think it is amazing that I am here. There must have been some master plan set in motion for me at that early age. God is at work here, and no doubt I'm in the right place. I just really, really relate to these children. I feel like I know what they're feeling. My heart goes out to these children because they have had such horrific lives and endured unbearable pain.

We have created some of our own foster and group homes—not nearly enough, though, to handle the amount of children who come through the Childhelp Villages. Sara, Yvonne, and the volunteers keep working to raise funds in hopes of creating more. I've never seen a more devoted Board of Directors.

We get a number of children who have turned their pain inwards. Their environments have been so terrible that in some cases, I am even surprised that they were able to make it. These children have had to keep silent about their situation for protection. Most of them have been led to believe they are no good and therefore form a pattern of punishing themselves. I can't believe the degree of damage that has been done to some of these children.

"Why?" I keep asking.

And I have yet to find a justifiable answer. There isn't one, as far as I'm concerned. No child deserves this kind of treatment. To rip the innocence from a child is beyond my comprehension.

I have witnessed time and time again that Childhelp is a wonderful place for these children, and I believe it's the best years of their life. We work hard to give the children some life skills so that they can make it on the outside. I see that it's a very positive place where these children can find some direction in dealing with their anger and a degree of understanding about what's happened to them. We consider it a success if they can come to learn that they're not a bad person and that they are worth caring about. For most, it is the first time they start to believe they have a right to be here, be alive, and have some happiness and safekeeping. It is the first time in their young lives that they begin to believe they have any value at all.

We should all be very grateful there is a place of healing love like Childhelp provides.

don't look at me

A STAFF MEMBER SHARES
THE STORY OF BRANDON

Brandon was a young boy who came to Childhelp Village in one of the worst physical conditions from abuse that I had ever seen. I am a nurse here who has seen a lot. Yet it is difficult for me to even tell this story. I can only thank God that he made it here.

As the story goes, when he was an infant in his crib, if he cried too much, his father would slice his face with a razor blade. By the time Brandon came to us for treatment, he was so disfigured that he had grown his hair long and combed it forward to cover his face. He constantly kept his head down because he was embarrassed and had come to the belief that no one could possibly want him—or love him. Brandon was so withdrawn that he rarely spoke. Over the course of several years, we tried everything we knew to try to get him to talk but he wouldn't; he was afraid to make a sound. One of his therapies took him to visit the animals at least once a week, but he never said anything there either.

Sara and Yvonne were able to get a friend, Dr. Ed Terino,

to arrange plastic surgery in an effort to rebuild his nose, ears, and the deep scars on his face. It took a lot of loving coaching from Sara and Yvonne to even get Brandon to consider it. You see, he had been taken through many, many emergency rooms as a child because of his father's abuse that he was convinced that going to any hospital meant something bad would be connected. It was the extra love and care that Sara and Yvonne gave to him that would eventually bring him to a point of ease where he would have the courage to agree to go. They told Brandon that they would go with him, stay with him, and not leave him alone through each operation. And they did! It was amazing to watch them taking shifts staying night and day in his hospital room. This went on through several surgeries over a few years. "The Ladies" would be there each time with balloons and hugs to show him how proud they were of him.

It was during this whole process of healing and reconstructive surgery that a miracle happened. A local married couple, the Smiths, who volunteered as Special Friends at the Village fell in love with Brandon.

Brandon so longed to be adopted that he was quickly drawn to the Smiths by the love they exhibited toward him. The two of them came to see him as often as possible and became his extended family. They let him know they loved him and talked about the possibility of his coming to live with them someday. Of course, this was a dream beyond his imagining at the time.

Think how exciting it must have been for that little boy who had never felt love in his life. What I have learned from being with these children is that if they don't have respect and love at home, they start to lose all hope. Up until that time, Brandon had very little hope left in his life.

One day, Brandon was down at the ranch and was petting one of the sheep he had become close to. Her name was Gennie. As usual, the therapist and I were keeping one eye and ear trained on him in hopes of hearing some sound from the boy. By now he was about 11 and would rarely speak out—most times only giving a nod of his head.

Then suddenly, out of nowhere, we heard, "Gennie, do you know that I love the Smiths? I want to be their son."

When word spread about what had happened, everyone at Childhelp was in tears.

From that point forward, Brandon began to open up. As his face healed from the surgeries, he became more outgoing. I never will forget his last Christmas with us. He had blossomed into such a talkative young boy that he was doing a part in the pageant. I can still remember sitting in the front row with tears uncontrollably rolling down my face as I looked at him up on the stage. There was this beautiful child who in the past rarely lifted his head, or looked anyone in the eye, or even spoke, standing stage center in the Christmas pageant, looking out at the audience with a smile on his face, searching for Sara and Yvonne and the Smiths, and singing Christmas carols at the top of his lungs as if he'd been doing it all his life.

That was one of the best Christmas presents I have ever had. And the best Christmas present Brandon ever had was that the Smiths *did* adopt him. He went on to graduate from high school, then on to college, and is now a fully functional member of society. I would have found it hard to believe all of that if I hadn't seen it with my own eyes. It just goes to show the power of love. This swells my heart with gratitude and joy when I recall this story. Imagine complete strangers falling in love with a little boy whose face was so disfigured that it was all most people could do just to look at him.

colin's story

AS TOLD BY A VILLAGE NURSE

We have one little boy, Colin, who, when he came here, was so withdrawn and developmentally delayed. He was really pretty much a "feral" child—like the animals he was raised around. He didn't know how to eat right and slept on the floor—that sort of thing. No one knows who his father is, and his mother had been incarcerated. He was originally put in a foster home by Social Services, but he wasn't able to do well. His foster parents couldn't bond with him due to his intense shyness, and so he ultimately came to us.

He was terribly detached and unresponsive when he first came that we all questioned just how much we could help him. Nevertheless, we would not give up hope of having some degree of impact on his healing. That morning, I was taking his blood pressure and put the cuff on his arm. I always let the children pump up the cuff themselves. I try to allow them some control in a situation whenever I can. I handed the pump to Colin as usual. We had been doing this for a while, so he has become accustomed to the procedure. Even so, he would rarely look me in the eyes and totally withdrew when he saw a needle. This, we suspected, had something to do with seeing his parents use them for their drugs. He would just take the pump and go through the routine.

One morning I was standing next to him, waiting for him to do his part so I could continue with the blood pressure check.

All of a sudden he stopped, looked up to me, opened his mouth, and asked, "To 140?" Just as clear as a bell.

I replied, "That's right, Colin."

My heart raced. I thought we were going to break-through. Maybe he was beginning to trust enough to start walking out of his withdrawn place of existence. When I was finished, I gave him a hug and almost danced out of the place. Later in the morning, I heard from his therapist that Colin, who would always hide when he saw him enter the cottage, came over to him and said, "Hello, doctor."

This was a child who just has absolutely bloomed here. He came here when he was four, and he's eight now. He's lived here half his life. Living at the Village is starting to create a life with new memories—memories of people who love him and have taken care of him. This was another lesson for me to never, *ever* think of giving up on one of these precious chil-dren. What we do here—well, for me—when I go home at night, I have a great feeling in my heart because I know we do great things while these children are here. I just wish we could keep them all until they are adults. Then they still would have the benefit of remaining under our umbrella—a philosophy and care they have come to know and trust: one that is totally focused on their healing and growth of self-esteem. I know Sara, Yvonne, and everyone connected to Childhelp are dili-gently working to accomplish that.

It would be perfect if every child who graduates from our villages could move directly into one of our group or foster homes.

Having fun while learning to trust.

Best friends.

Learning to follow directions.

Even some of the animals that came to the ranch have known abuse. The children seem to identify and shower love on them.

healing through animals

A RANCH WORKER'S WAY OF HEALING

On her first day at the ranch, Margaret was instructed to choose any animal that she wanted to work with. Margaret is an 8-year-old who lives at the Village. She came to the ranch program with no prior experience around animals. She was quite fearful of all the animals—even the small dogs. Her therapist recommended the ranch as an ideal way for Margaret to learn how to deal with her fears in a positive manner. Acknowledging her fear of the animals was the first step for Margaret in overcoming her fears in other areas of her life. Of course, she chose one of the small dogs, which was much less intimidating than any of the larger animals, including the horses.

Initially, every time the dog would move, Margaret would step back in fear. This child would actually jump back because she didn't know what the dog was going to do. However, through coaxing and reassurance that the dog would not harm her in any way, Margaret was eventually able to brush the dog thoroughly and take it for a walk without once turning away in fear. This began to increase Margaret's self-confidence and allowed her to move on to some of the larger animals. After several sessions with the dog, Margaret was told that it was time to learn about the horses. At first she was hesitant and didn't really want to even go near the horses, much less brush them. To ease her fears, Margaret was given one of the ponies to work with, as they are less intimidating than the larger horses merely because of their size.

After two sessions of brushing and getting acquainted with the pony, Margaret took it for a walk around the arena. Initially, Margaret would only hold the very end of the lead line while her instructor actually led the horse around. Each time the horse would try to turn around or trot, Margaret would drop the lead line and run the other direction. However, by the third session of taking the pony for a walk, Margaret was able to lead the pony on her own with confidence and gained the ability to redirect the pony if it tried to trot or turn around. As Margaret took the pony for a walk around the arena, she glowed with self-confidence. And she would stand for periods of time just letting the pony eat the grass in the warm summer sun.

By her third month at the ranch, Margaret's self confidence had increased enough for her to begin riding one of the horses. Even though Margaret had become much more relaxed and at ease around the animals by then, she was still nervous about getting on such a large animal. Overcoming her fears of the smaller animals became stepping-stones for Margaret and allowed her the ability and confidence to approach the horse, get on, and ride around—even if it was only for a brief amount of time. At first, Margaret said she just wanted to sit on the horse and didn't want the horse to move at all. With all the patience in the world, the horse just stood there for Margaret, letting her become adjusted to the sensation of sitting on top of such a large creature.

The animals here are really incredible with the children. Eventually, with encouragement and reassurance, Margaret was instructed to walk the horse around in small circles. As the horse began to walk, Margaret voiced her feelings of fear that she was going to fall off. Once again, I reassured her and walked along beside the horse holding Margaret's hand. She was told to walk the horse around in eight circles because she was eight years old. She was also told that she would only have to do the eight circles in one direction. But by the time she finished the first eight circles, Margaret had let go of my hand and said that she wanted to ride for eight more circles. To my amazement, when she finished that set, she turned the horse around and rode two more sets of eight circles in the opposite direction.

The smile on Margaret's face at the end of her first ride clearly illustrated how she had enjoyed herself and that she was well on the road to dealing with her fears in a healthy and happy process. Since her first day at the ranch, Margaret has developed an attitude of self-acceptance, along with increased self-confidence. She has also displayed the ability to overcome her fears in other areas of her life. She continues to come to the ranch and now comes with a buddy. Margaret assists her buddy and encourages her to work through her fears of some of the animals. Margaret has become a great joy to have at the ranch. That's just one of the success stories of how working with the animals at the ranch has affected the children.

The ranch and the animals provide a great avenue for the children to open up and begin to trust. It's amazing how they can bond with an animal quite often before they can allow themselves to do so with a human. In their minds, most people they have known in their young lives can't be trusted. With some of the children, there is such a deeply cemented resistance to attachment that it takes concentrated effort to accomplish some trust within that child again. Sometimes we get lucky, and that's what keeps us all going. That is why we are very creative here in our therapeutic approaches using the ranch, art, and spirituality coupled with traditional methods. What is constant in the forefront of my mind and therapy is to help each child learn that they have a degree of power—the power to make their own decisions in their best interests and safety, and the power to say "no."

When I came here, I was thrilled because I knew from the moment I walked in that I was in the right place. I found in one place all the things that were important to the recovery of abused children.

One of the first things that I experienced was when this child, Garrett, was down one day riding and I was giving him directions to follow while he was riding. He kept ignoring how I was instructing him to guide his horse and then became very frustrated because his horse wasn't following his directions.

The therapeutic part came afterward when I asked, "How did that feel when the horse wasn't following your directions?"

He explained that he was frustrated and angry.

I inquired, "Do you think maybe you can understand why that was happening? Were you really listening and following the directions that I was giving you?"

"Well, no."

And so he came to understand the feeling of frustration that happens when people aren't listening. And you know, that's really difficult to explain to young children, but when you experience it, you get it.

I said, "Do you think maybe you could cause that in other people when you don't listen? Do you think you might understand better now how that feels?"

He responded, "Yeah."

I told him: "Maybe the next time you can think what you might do differently."

And he concluded, "Well, maybe I'll follow your directions."

He did the next time, the horse followed his directions, and it was a much better ride.

I have a variety of programs. I have a feeding program where some of the children come down to feed the animals. They have to be on a certain level so they're a little more independent, a little more responsible. They come down and they help me feed and water the animals, and they actually get an allowance for that. After they have done one chore for a while, the children are then allowed to stay with that one or change their responsibilities. We present them with the opportunity for making their own choices—their own decisions. If they decide to move on to something else, they must then go through a process of giving notice and finishing out a period of time until someone else takes their place. This helps them learn about how to be responsible.

When they feel they are complete with a certain chore and ready to change, they say their good-byes to the animal and take the responsibility to show the next child coming in what to do with the animal they are caring for or the chore they are performing for that animal. A lot of the children who come down here stay connected in some way with the ranch until they leave the Village. And that is really wonderful for me to see. It just validates how important this all is in terms of their growth and self-esteem. One of the other by-products of the ranch is that these children who are, for the most part, under-nourished, under-loved, and under-cared for learn to create that atmosphere themselves through the animals.

One of our greatest stories is about a little boy who was born with cocaine in his system and had been a severe victim of neglect by his mother. He had been moved back and forth between his grandmother and mother until being placed in a county foster home where he had been physically abused. He was briefly returned to his mother and then back with his grandmother and was removed and placed in foster care again as his behaviors became uncontrollable. He went back to the grandmother again, and again, due to behaviors, was removed to a group home. It was requested that he be moved to the Village because he was a lot younger at that time than the other children at his placement. His mother was eventually incarcerated for burglary and was not granted any visitation. She was a chronic drug user, and his father had apparently abused him sexually. Obviously, neither one of his parents were really involved in his life.

This boy, I'll call him "Josh," displayed concerns of trust and abandonment, as well as suffered from low self-esteem and a lack of confidence in his own abilities. He also had poor relationship skills with his peers and with adults. His therapist, in hopes that he would develop self-confidence and improve his relationship skills, recommended that he come to the Village ranch. He did not exhibit any unusual fears of the animals. In fact, he seemed relaxed and at ease around them.

When Josh first started coming to the ranch, he was assigned tasks such as feeding and caring for the animals. Of course, initially, Josh just wanted to ride and wasn't really into caring for the animals. However, he was told that if he would do his job on a regular basis, he would be rewarded with an occasional ride. That worked for him. Soon he was not only looking forward to riding but also actually began to enjoy taking care of the animals. He was even beginning to anticipate their needs just through observation. By observing the animals responding to him with their soft snickers of anticipation when he came down to feed, Josh soon began to recognize that the animals actually depended on him to feed and care for them.

One day, I asked how Josh thought they would feel if he did not feed them. He said he thought they would be sad. He started coming to the ranch twice a week, once to feed and once to ride the horses. Josh was always observant and had a memory that was sharp, always remembering what he learned about the animals, and then applying this each time he rode. He was soon developing relationships with the animals at the ranch. He was learning to trust and be trusted by behaving in a consistent manner and observing that the horses' response to him was always positive. Josh developed close relationships with a couple of horses. He knew their individual personalities, along with their idiosyncrasies and treated them accordingly.

For example, one horse was a lush for attention. Josh lavished her with lots of affection by brushing and hugging her each time he came to the ranch. On occasion, the horse would try Josh's patience when he rode her. Once in a while, Josh forgot to apply patience and yelled at the horse; however, on his own, Josh always apologized and continued to care for the horse after the ride, giving her hugs and kisses before putting her away. Thanks to his relationship with the animals, Josh improved his relationship skills with his peers and no longer had problems with being abusive toward anyone.

Josh had a younger buddy who came to the ranch with him once a week to ride. Oddly enough, his buddy had experienced a very similar background of abuse. Josh assumed a sort of mentor role with this younger buddy and assisted him without being too bossy or demeaning. Josh displayed patience and understanding of his younger buddy who grew to look up to Josh with respect. That had also contributed to an increased self-esteem for Josh. Josh became one of the model children at the ranch. He was one of the best riders and also learned how to care for each and every animal at the ranch.

These are only a few of my stories of the magic that happens here at the Childhelp Village ranch. There are so many more. It is really great to be a part of this crusade to break the silence that has shrouded this epidemic of abuse that children are suffering. It is wonderful to be a part of something that brings hope and healing to these children.

The healing that happens at the ranch with the children is because they're outside and the animals pose no real threat. It is a great tool to couple with the traditional therapy they get here at the Village. They don't think of it as therapy. They think of it more as fun, and they enjoy it. And they actually get certain needs met—that need for attention and affection—from the animals. I also think that for them to start healing, it's important that they start to care about—or for—something. For them to actually start taking care of an animal opens the door so that they can heal the void inside themselves.

Some of the animals we have here at the ranch have been abused also—just like the children—and they can identify with that. We had a cow that had been severely injured when someone had thrown acid on him. He had been a prize steer and this boy had done that because he was jealous of his owner, another boy, who won all the top awards at the 4H Club. The children loved that cow. And he would let five or six at a time ride on him. We also had a pony that was partially deformed. The children seem to sense that they have gone through similar abuse. It is awesome to watch the children shower love on the animals and get it back in return every time. We even had a goat that learned to go up the road to where the bus dropped the children off after school. He was there every afternoon to meet them—right on time. Then he walked them back to their individual cottages.

Horses have been a big part of my life. In caring for them, they have in turn cared for me. I watch the transformations that happen when the children connect with them and the rest of the animals. It happens over and over again. The children know how the animals feel about them after awhile, and later they come to realize somewhere inside what that animal has done for them. They may not be able to verbalize it, but somehow they all know they are receiving love unconditionally.

don't turn out the lights

SARA TALKS ABOUT STRETCHING THE RULES

There was one little boy, Stephen, who came to us from a rural community. When his parents were angry and wanted to punish him, he was buried alive again and again in a pit they had dug in their backyard. They would make him lie down in it and then shovel dirt over him. The only reason he had not suffocated was that they were "kind" enough to put a straw in his mouth for him to breathe.

His parents would then play a game, placing bets with each other as to whether he would live. We found out that this had gone on for a couple of years. One evening, however, a neighbor walking nearby heard his muffled screams and called the authorities, who, in turn, came and arrested them. Stephen was sent to social services. That's how he came to us.

When Stephen first arrived, he never wanted the lights to be turned off in his bedroom or the hallway. Also, no matter how cold it was, this sweet child would push the covers down at night and lie shivering because having the weight of the blankets on him triggered the memory of being buried in the pit. He simply would not go to sleep without these things done. He had nightmares practically every night and would wake up screaming and gasping for breath. This went on for months, and we were beside ourselves about what to do.

And then there came divine intervention.

We got this new puppy that was just a little over six weeks old at the Village. He would scamper all over the cottage, and Stephen came to love him and show him great attention. One night, we were putting the children to bed with the puppy following behind. As we came to Stephen's room, the puppy saw him, jumped right up on his bed, and started licking him in the face. Stephen was ecstatic with joy and asked if the puppy could sleep with him.

We don't usually allow the children to sleep with any of the animals, but we made an exception that night. Sometimes you just have to take a chance that to step outside the rules might have some positive effect. This night it did. Stephen slept through the night for the first time, so the puppy was allowed to sleep with him until he eventually overcame his fear of the dark.

He now sleeps with the lights out, joyously cocooned in his blankets.

The inside world of
an abused child is revealed through art.

Art is transforming.

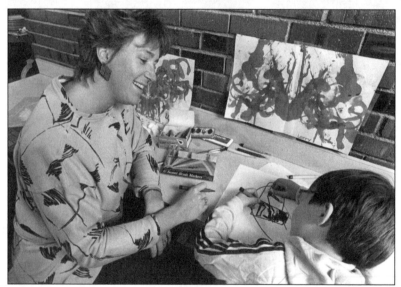

The healing begins.

CHAPTER NINE

art illustrating life

TRANSFORMATION
THROUGH CREATIVE EXPRESSION

We didn't know very much about Tommy's history when he came to us. No one could get him to open up and talk. He was about six and had an assigned general therapist here at the Village. She thought that maybe doing art might help, so she asked if she could try bringing him over to the studio here.

"Sure," I said, "Why not?"

I decided that I would have the young boy create a large image of himself. When he arrived, I took a piece of butcher paper that was cut to his height and tacked it to a wall. Then I had him stand against it and carefully drew an outline of his own body. As we stepped back, I asked Tommy to draw anything he wanted to help describe to me who he was and what he was about. He took one of the markers and began working on it.

At first there was hair, next eyes, a nose, and a mouth. He was meticulous about what he was creating. Then he stopped for a moment and just stared at the picture. Next thing I knew he walked forward and drew genitals, after which, he began to laugh as if he thought this was very funny. I said nothing. Just observed. Then he abruptly stopped the laughing and became silent, almost as if embarrassed by his display, and began scribbling with the marker to try to cover over what he had drawn.

I knew we had hit on something, and so I discussed it with his therapist. She brought him down the next day, and together we asked him to talk about what his picture meant to him. Within minutes we were able to break the silence on that fact that his mother had been molesting him for as long as he could remember. This would not be the only time I would hear a story like this over the years to come, yet it is always much more painful to hear when you know that the parent was the perpetrator. Parents are supposed to be the protector.

This was one of the first encounters I had when I came to Childhelp Village.

The great thing about using art for healing is that it reconnects the child to a world that is limitless. Whatever a child chooses to use as his or her form of expression and what he or she ultimately creates provides a record of his or her personality and how he or she sees the world they live in. The more horrifying their life has been, the more abstract the artistic expression. Their art becomes their biography. In art, the children learn to have some degree of control for the first time in a life that has most often been out of control. This is where they can take the chaos they have known and begin to move it into something manageable.

When the children come to do art projects of any kind—whether it be drawing, working with clay, creating stories and performances of their own, reading, writing, or any other means of expression—they cannot fail. Using art with the children here has proven to be a collaboration between them and God. Everything they create is done with great feeling, even if those feelings are below the visible surface at first. Whatever they are creating is really not about the object outside of themselves that is being "born"; it is about that silent dialogue that is going inside their minds and hearts.

I first just try to open up the children to all the possibilities they can have to create then allow them to be drawn in whatever direction and to whatever medium that is inherent to them. All children are artists of some kind. We just usually expose them to what we have here, and then let them take the lead. I always love watching a child's eyes light up when he or she discovers or connects to something that "rings" for him or her.

Many of the children who come to the art room are incredibly withdrawn and silent. They do not wish to discuss or open up about their lives before arriving at the Village— like Tommy. It is too painful. For many, coming here is the first time there has been any relief from the abuse they have been experiencing. We are trained to study their history and then keep our awareness heightened.

You never know when that moment will come when "the hidden secret" will start to expose itself. Then hopefully, we will at some point recognize when a child begins to crack open that well preserved outer-shell, and the healing process can begin. It is heartbreaking to see how much these precious beings carry in their troubled souls. So much, at such a young age. It often seems that the child who is the most creative in a family is the one who suffers the most. Usually, it is because that child is the one who questions and wonders more than the other children in the family, and they also tend to remember with more detail what is happening at the time.

All the facets of their home life give reason to why most of the children who come here have trouble with routine and authority figures. First of, there has been little or no routine in their lives. Second, the adult figures have been causing the abuse. It often takes awhile before they can settle into the routine here and quite often even longer to adjust to any degree of trust around the adults.

I remember one little girl who was quite shy. Angeline is her name, and she was 11. She was not the leader in any of my groups. She didn't exhibit any rebellious or destructive outbursts. In the beginning, she rarely talked. She always wanted to stay in the background of any activity going on with the other children. I brought her over to the art room, and we began working with paints. She liked to mix the colors—got really involved in doing that. She was fascinated by how mixing different hues would change the color. Some days that would be all we would do. She had not been doing well in school. She wouldn't do her homework, and if she did, she wouldn't take it in to class. But when we were in this one-on-one situation mixing paints, she started to open up and communicate verbally.

Soon, Angeline became drawn exclusively to painting. She would spend great amounts of time mixing her paints before the actual painting would begin. Once she began to paint on the art paper, it was like she had discovered a private place that was all her own. She was a natural. She would just create these wonderful characters that came out of some inner reservoir that were abstract at first, but so exquisitely defined. She produced many different characters. But a majority of the time, her paintings were of clowns. They would have these huge sad eyes, sometimes they were crying, and most often possessed distorted features. When I would compliment her, she would say that the characters she drew were all of herself. Never anyone else—no parents, no siblings. There was deep melancholy that came through these extraordinary paintings.

Periodically, I would have these little art shows for the children to show their work. I save most everything the children did. For the longest time, Angeline asked to not have any of hers exhibited. I honored that. The first sign I recognized that something was shifting with her was when she asked if she could cut up her pictures and create new ones out of the pieces. This told me she was beginning to integrate all the parts of herself she had kept separate. As much as I hated to see these pictures destroyed, I knew out of the destruction was about to come a "new" Angeline. The journey of recreating herself began. It took a couple of weeks of sessions for her to complete her collage. But when it was through, the image that had blossomed forth was amazing. It was a happier image, and one she was proud of. In fact, when she was finished, she announced that I could put this portrait in the next art show. This experience had been transforming for both of us. For Angeline, art became a language of her own. For me, I recognize the power of this medium of healing. It had given her a voice where before there had been silence.

She eventually developed relationships with another little girl here, and they became best friends. The two would come to the art room and spend hours painting and making sculptures. They would use wood and glue and make these incredible art pieces. I still have one of them in my office now. When it came time for Angeline to leave the Village, I gave her a paint set as a goodbye gift. It was really hard to see her go. Yet she was going to a wonderful family who we all knew loved her, and she was happy with them.

We have heard many, many times that "art imitates life." But through the years of working here, I have discovered that quite often life is so poignantly illustrated through art. In many cases, that provides an enormous healing process. I have been grateful that Sara and Yvonne incorporated art into the programs of Childhelp—and have done so from the very beginning of the Villages.

Art has proven to be a magnificent tool of healing with these children. I think the best thing we can ever hope for in our work is to give the children back to themselves. We can't go with them when they leave, although you may want to with those you grow especially close to, and many times you lose contact. That's the hard part. But with God's help and this wonderful place, we can give them the strength to go on and feel good about themselves. They are not bad children; they have just had bad things happen to them. The joy of seeing the "lights go on" behind their darkened eyes is a joy that I will carry with me always.

One day, about ten years after Angeline had left, I got a phone call from her. She was going on vacation with some friends and would be coming by the Village. She was now about to be 21 and wanted to know if she could stop by and visit.

Of course, I was elated and answered, "Yes!"

When she arrived, we all did a swift walk around the property. Then Angeline asked to go to the art room alone with me. There before me was this lovely young woman, still a bit shy. First, I took her through my office to show her I still had the sculpture she had created. As we entered the main room, she stood silent for a minute and then began to cry.

"Are you okay, darlin," I said—I wasn't prepared for this.

After a few moments that felt like a lifetime, the silence broke, she turned to me, and said, "Oh, yes. Yes, I'm *very* okay. I just had to come in here with you to say thanks. You see, this is the room that saved my life."

amy's story

CREATIVE REDIRECTION

They didn't just abuse her body. They also managed to frighten her spirit with threats that the devil would get her. When Amy came to the Village, she was afraid to close her eyes and go to sleep at night; she thought the devil would come and harm her. No matter how exhausted she was, her fear awakened her many times during the night.

On one occasion, I asked Amy to tell me everything she knew about this terrible devil. She showed me a knot in the wood on top of her nightstand.

"This is where the devil sits," she informed me. "He's six inches tall with a real mean face, and he hangs his feet down over the edge, right here."

She said he was bright red, and he watched her in bed all night long.

While working with the rest of the staff, I gave Amy a 12-inch-tall angel doll that would sit on her nightstand, covering up the demonic knot.

"Devils are uncomfortable with angels," I told her, "so

he probably won't come back anymore."

"That's a cool trick to play on the devil," Amy said with a smile and promptly named her angel doll "Angela." That night, with Angela propped on her nightstand, Amy snuggled into bed in her room that she shared with two other girls, confident that she was safe from the devil. After a few minutes, she got up and turned Angela around so she was watching over all three beds.

"We don't want the devil coming and scaring the other girls either," Amy stated to me.

For the first time in her short life, Amy closed her eyes, dropped right off to sleep without hesitation, and slept through the entire night without once waking up.

This, of course, was only a place to start with Amy. Our treatment team began working to break her dependency on a doll for her sense of safety, helping her to identify and reduce her fears until she was secure enough to fall asleep on her own. That day did come. Until it did, Angela's watch over Amy provided the comfort and safety she needed to feel in order to get the rest the dear child needed—and deserved.

CHAPTER TEN

why we do
what we do

A VILLAGE ADMINISTRATOR
SPEAKS ABOUT COMMITMENT

"Do you have an appointment?" the receptionist asked. "Most of our tours are scheduled."

"Well, no," the young man replied, "but I used to live here."

It was around Christmas time, and my assistant and I were standing up at the front desk of the Village of Childhelp West in Beaumont discussing the day as we looked over some paperwork. Both of us had been at the Village for over 17 years. The main door opened as this young man, who looked to be in his mid to late 20s, accompanied by two young ladies, came in walking toward us. He had made a sharp turn and walked directly to the receptionist asking if he could have a tour.

Upon hearing this, I walked over to him and inquired, "Well, young man, what is your name?"

"Jeremy," he announced proudly. "Jeremy."

I was thinking, *Jeremy . . . Jeremy.*

I looked over at my assistant, and she was doubled over, laughing hysterically. "Jeremy?" she said.

He kind of shook his head, his face started to spread into a wide smile. All of a sudden, my memory was sparked. Then I started laughing. My mind was on a fast rewind as I began to remember this young man as a boy.

"Oh, now I remember you. You were on every rooftop of every building. You were always running, and I would chase you all over the property trying to catch you. You certainly gave me a workout. I was always taking care of scrapes and bruises from climbing after you to get you down. Oh, yes, Jeremy, I remember you *very* well."

Jeremy just stood there, his head slightly turned down, as a red blush spread over his face. Of course, the girls with him were all giggles as they noticed his reaction. He then proceeded to introduce us to one of the girls as his fiancée and the other as her girlfriend.

"And just what are you doing here, Jeremy?"

"Well, I'm a fireman now and about to be married. I wanted to bring my fiancée to see the place that I called 'home.' It was an important time and an important part of my life."

All I could say was, "Oh, I see. Then I think your fiancée and her friend should see our place."

I didn't have time to take him on the tour, but I had my assistant take him. We parted with how nice it was to see each other again, and that it was great to see he was doing well. After the tour, when Jeremy left, my assistant and I agreed how heartwarming it was to see something like this because the Village is a great part of so many children's childhood. It is an important part. It is part of the good memories that many of our children retain. It can override the horrible abuse they have suffered. We work hard to create a safe and loving atmosphere. That's why it is heartwarming for us when anyone returns and brings the people they are close to now to show them what they learned and held dear at this place they learned to call "home." I feel so proud and blessed to be a part of what we are doing. We have changed lives, and Jeremy is one of our miracles.

Here's another miracle: There is one girl from here who calls about every two months or so just to check in. She is happily married and has three children of her own. She broke the cycle of abuse in her life. When she left here, the courts determined to send her home. Her dad had re-abused her. But she spoke up, as she was taught here to do, and that broke the cycle. She was removed permanently from the home. Now that's a great success story.

I have been with the Village in Beaumont for 17 years. I spent the first few years working directly with the children in the cottages, most of those years as a cottage supervisor. From there about seven years ago, I moved up to the administration building. We have about 80 children at any given time. The children who come here are usually court-dependent. They have failed at five or six placements before they come to us.

A typical scenario for one of these children might be that the parents are making methamphetamines. The police come, remove the children, and put them in shelter care. They then look for family members who would be willing to take them. The children go to family members, the children act out, the family members are stressed with their own life, and eventually the county social worker removes them, placing them with a foster home.

The children, for various reasons that are really understandable, become angry. They're scared, and they become rebellious because of being in a situation with several other children with problems. A child might become suicidal or bent toward doing some kind of self-inflicted harm to himself or herself. No one seems to be able to either handle them or want them. That's generally when they come to the Village. It is horrible what some of these children have been through.

There are approximately 115 to 120 staff members here on-site at the Beaumont Village. They come from a wide variety of backgrounds. We have a maintenance crew, a housekeeping crew, child-care workers who work directly with the children, animal therapists, a full-time chaplain, clinical coordinators, therapists, a librarian, kitchen staff, as well as a whole variety of other support staff. The librarian heads our literacy program, and there's the ranch with its animal programs. We also have a wonderful group of volunteers who do various things with—and for—the children. The list just goes on and on. Of course, it is always beneficial when someone comes with a history of working with children like we have here. They are all wonderful people at heart and want to be here. They understand that these children have particular needs because of what has happened in their lives. That is extremely important.

We have our own exclusive education schools on property to teach those children who are not qualified to attend public schools. Some children come without any testing whatsoever. Sometimes it comes down to the simplest of things like no one ever told them that the grass is *green*, and the sky is *blue*—basic things that every child should know. They have no idea, but it's amazing the progress—a miracle really—and the growth they make once they've been here for a short period of time. They've just never been exposed to any kind of structured learning. No one's read them stories. Nobody taught them their numbers. That's really incomprehensible and amazing for any of us to observe. No one has given them real caring love.

The unfortunate part is that most of the children have come from such chaos that they've not done *anything* at a consistent level. They haven't had consistent medical care. They haven't gone to school on a consistent basis. There has been little to nonexistent consistency in their young lives. And we go through all sorts of challenges to find out what is most appropriate for them. Usually the most they have seen of anything consistent is the abuse they have had to suffer. Sometimes they are really frightened because of what has happened in their lives. The reasons stem from being so often told that they are bad children; therefore, they want to rid themselves of the "bad" within them. Some might have a problem with stealing, and a lot of them have very foul language. They haven't known any other language than what they have heard at home.

When the children first arrive, they get a used bike. For their birthday or Christmas, whichever comes first, they get a new bike. Everything they get here, from clothing to bikes to toys, is theirs to take with them when they move on. Their initials are placed on everything. For many, it is the first time that they have *anything* to call their own. It has proven to be good to have as many activities as we do, and giving them their own possessions helps instill a sense of responsibility.

It's heartbreaking to know that for many of these children, the first young years of their lives have been spent diving in and out of dumpsters for food with their brothers and sisters. We had one child who had been doing that since seven years old to feed himself and his siblings. It's also hard to look into the eyes of a child who has been exposed to drugs and/or alcohol pre-birth. They come into life at a disadvantage. Many parents have a drug and/or alcohol abuse problem. Many are making their money through prostitution—and it's not just women. Oftentimes the moms have failed to protect the child. They may not have done the abuse themselves; however, they knew the dad was, or the grandpa, or the uncle, or the aunt, or the neighbor, or their boyfriend—and they looked the other way.

Many of these children's parents have been too drugged

out or drunk to prepare a meal, or maybe they don't even have food—so the children have found themselves on their own time and again. If you are a child with younger siblings, and you're only five or six, then you're doing whatever you can—stealing, begging, or diving in a dumpster in order to feed both yourself and your siblings. It's not that uncommon in these children's history. That's why when they come to us, 85 to 90 percent are developmentally delayed.

We feel a deep investment in these children and what they have experienced. We want them to learn more than just some survival skills. We want them to develop anger management skills, socialization skills; learn about spirituality; and undergo character-building programs. We feel this is what sets us apart from other programs. We realize that to build strong self-esteem has a long-lasting effect. Once they leave here, we want them to know what to do if something bad ever happens to them again. Most of them know we have an 800 number here. They generally do call back to say hello, tell us they're thinking about us, or just speak with friends. The people here at the Village often become the family they never had. It is known as "home" to them.

Sara and Yvonne established this first Childhelp Village in 1978. It does seem to be a pattern that when many of these children are just reaching their mid to late 20s, they begin to come to terms and to grips with their abuse. We've started getting a lot of calls and visits from ex-residents, just like the young man whom I opened this story with. When they do come back, quite often, I get to give them the tour. And it's incredible. For all of the children whom I have talked to who used to be here, this has remained one of the best parts of their childhood. They had the consistency, they had the routine, they had a roof over their heads, they had clothing, they had toys, and they felt the love—and they learned there is a God who loves them. The spiritual program is one of the priorities our founders put into place. They had everything they needed to *begin* to experience a safe and secure childhood. When I walk them around, it's beautiful just to see the expressions on their faces and hear their comments. It's like "this used to be my bed" or that maybe where they were housed is an all-boy cottage now, when it used to be for girls. Before we had our Activity Center, they did talent shows and those kinds of things on the steps right in front of the library.

Sometimes I'll hear, "We used to do talent shows here!"

And I'll reply, "Yeah, we did, didn't we?" It's just an incredible experience.

As part of my job, I oversee our volunteer programs. We have several groups that support us. They are called "Special Friends," "Angel Pals," and "Eagles." They are especially important to the children who have little or no visitations. Most of them have no one in their lives who care for them. These volunteer groups have various functions and spend time with the children to give them a positive male and female role model in their lives. We try to individualize these programs by connecting our children one-on-one with the role model that best suits their needs. A lot of these people have their own careers, families, and personal lives—yet they devote amazing amounts of time to supporting us and the children.

Special Friends have the opportunity to become involved with a child one-on-one. We also ask them to call the child at least once a month or to be available so the child can call them. If they would like to go a little bit further and want to come and visit more often, they certainly can. We are thrilled when that happens. If they'd like to take the children off grounds, like for shopping, or to lunch, there are a few more procedures they have to go through to be able to do that. We are committed to the protection and well-being of the child.

With Special Friends, it is especially difficult when it comes time for a child to leave and they have to sever ties as recommended by social services. The reality is that with the new family, the child is starting a new part of their life, yet both go through a process of grief and loss. After all, the child has been with them four or five years in some cases. It doesn't mean, however, that total knowledge of the child is necessarily lost. I have several volunteers who have followed the children's progress indirectly. There is one child whose soccer coach adopted him right here in Banning, and he's getting ready to graduate this year. He drives, plays on the football team, and gets good grades. He has been easy to follow. He's another miracle. There are success stories. But the problem is tracking them—the research part of that—due to the confidentiality.

That's why it's important to have all these volunteers. Whether they be groups like the men who fix the bikes, or the ladies who teach the children to enjoy the qualities found in gardening—growing, nurturing, responsibility, and the rewards that come from those things—or they come in and read to the children. They are all incredible and extremely important to the staff, the children, and Childhelp. It's all of them working together—beginning with our chapters and auxiliaries—that continue to have events all year long that helps keep our villages going.

It's amazing that when I go out to speak to groups, invariably, at least one person in any given group will come up later and admit, "I was abused as a child." It's very common. Many then become a volunteer in some way. The vast majority of people don't realize what a common and silent plight child abuse has been for so many years. I am grateful that *that* silence is being broken.

The first day that I drove through the gates, I just had this incredibly peaceful feeling. I was home. And it has not changed in 17 years. That day ignited a new passion and direction within me about what I was going to be doing with my life. I really have to believe this was God-sent in some way. How perfect. I could put my education to work with these children who had lived through a really hideous start in life.

I have many facets of my position here at Beaumont Village, and one I love is decorating the cottages to make sure that we have a warm and beautiful atmosphere for these children to call "home." I must say that our wonderful founders—"The Ladies," as we call them—started all the concepts and standards. They want this to be a comfortable environment that projects their philosophy that if one's surroundings are well maintained and inviting, a place that you are proud of and take part in, you will feel better about yourself and your self-esteem improves. I agree with that. I *totally* agree with that. I have a passion for what I do and the children who come here for healing.

Sara and Yvonne are incredible women. They're sincere. They're spiritual. There's hardly a time when they come out here and don't come to tears over hearing the story of a new child who has come into the Village. Even after all these years, they're not hardened, and they just continue to do a fabulous job for these children. What commitment! I just love my job. I love the organization, I love the volunteers, and I love the children. I've learned so much here.

A highway patrolman stopped one of our staff recently, and I guess he must have seen "Childhelp" posted somewhere on her car.

He said to her: "Oh, you work at Childhelp?"

She responded, "Yes."

"I used to live there," was his reply. And he let her go! So, you know there are many success stories out there.

Just a couple weeks ago, I went to one of the cottages to hang some pictures and put some pennants up on the wall— just to make sure that the cottage aesthetically looked really good. There was this one young boy who was coming down to get his pajamas to go take his shower to get ready for bed.

"Hey," he said.

"Hey," back I replied.

"Can I help you?" he asked.

I responded, "Sure." There we were busily hanging things on the wall. As I would hang, he would busily peel off the double stick tape.

Every few minutes or so he'd say, "Wow, we're just hanging out."

And I'd answer, "Well, yeah, yeah. We are. And doing some work, too."

He said, "I really like this."

We went into another bedroom, were working more in there, when he looked at me and told me: "You know you remind me of my mom."

I replied, "Really? In what way?"

There was this beautiful boy of about ten—blonde-haired, blue-eyed—and I was not sure what his answer would be. I didn't know if he was going to say, "Because you're tall," or "You have the same hair color," or whatever.

What he said after a moment's pause was, "Well, I don't really remember my mom. But if I had a mom, I would want her to be like you."

That just kind of choked me up and brought a little tear to my eye. About that time, one of the staff came in and said, "Hey! You're supposed to be in the shower!"

"Well, I'm hanging out with Lynn," he proudly announced. Even after all these years, you realize they can still touch your heart. I like that.

He saw me just a couple of nights ago as I walked in with one picture in my hand and he was eating dinner.

He quickly came over and asked, "Can I help you?"

I replied, "I just have to hang one picture."

And he went on to say, "Lynn, thank you for the Pokémon cards."

I had written him a little thank you because he really was a big help that evening and had enclosed a packet of Pokémon cards.

"Maybe the next time you come, and I help you, can I get some more Pokémon cards?"

My first thought was, *What a typical child.* And then I thought, *Nothing is typical about the children who come here in resemblance to other children—at first.* To see this was an instant reminder of what we do here. A grin spread over my face as I left the room.

Our goal here is to help these children heal—grow, stabilize, and learn. They won't forget what has happened to them. Some will need some kind of ongoing therapy for quite awhile. But if we can do everything we can to offer them a safe and loving atmosphere, supported by professionals who care—replace some of the elements of their former chaotic existence—we find that they generally respond very well. Most of them are developmentally delayed somewhere— whether academically, with their social skills, in their hand-eye coordination, or with any number of other aspects of their lives. We concentrate on all those areas. Everything we do here is therapeutic in some way. It is all focused on healing that innocent child within. We all believe that every child who comes here still has some small place inside that has not been touched or harmed by his or her unfortunate existence. We are committed to finding that "special place" and revealing it to the child. The Village is about creating miracles. It's amazing to think that this place could not have happened if it had not been for Sara and Yvonne and other open hearts.

anything is possible

A YOUNG MAN TALKS ABOUT HIS NEW LEASE ON LIFE

I was ten years old when I came to Childhelp Village. My life to that point had been like a ping pong ball, bouncing back and forth living with my mom, older sister, and brother when I was not in some detention home. I had a younger half-brother who lived with my biological dad in another state, but I had never met him and rarely saw my father. My older brother was a half-brother by another man with my mom, and my sister and I were from the same father. So, I was the youngest in our immediate family.

I had been in several group homes, and nothing was working. I was always getting in trouble. I know now that what I was suffering from, which had gone undiagnosed at the time, was ADD—attention deficit disorder. No one knew much about it back then in the late '80s. Of course, there were feelings embedded deep inside me that fueled my disorder. But I wouldn't become aware of those for some years to come.

My mom had to work a lot. So when I was at home, a lot of the time, my siblings and I were usually by ourselves. I don't believe that Mom didn't care about us. It was just that she had to work, and her focus was on making enough for us to live. I was very shy when I was younger—still am really—and felt no one understood me. When my attention toward my mom was rejected, I usually just wanted to be left alone. But that didn't happen very often. I was always acting out and getting in trouble or getting expelled from school. It was very frustrating for my mom. None of the children wanted to hang out with me, so I turned on them. I now believe that was because I really wanted someone to notice that I was alive. I felt very out-of-sorts with most everything. And I didn't like adults very much at all. They just always seemed to be telling me what to do or reaffirming that I was a troublemaker—no good. I really didn't see why I had to go to school at all.

No one seemed to care or understand what I felt, and I wasn't sure what I felt most of the time. Just many days of being confused and sad. I know that I felt very much alone in my early years. I began my life in homes and institutions at the early age of seven. I became a repeat run-away by the age of nine. I just felt that I didn't belong anywhere. I must be some kind of mistake.

My mother even moved us from place to place trying to regroup, restart, and outrun our growing reputation as a troubled family. We had finally settled once again in a small town in California, where my mom's dad lived, and we were doing fine for a while. Then it all broke apart. One day I had spewed out some unsavory dialogue toward my teacher and threw my book at her. The principal came and got me and said that he was going to take me home and have a long talk with my mom about whether I should come back to that school or not. He had had enough.

Many days of upset for my mom followed. Before I knew it, we were off again, this time moving all the way East to a small town in Virginia. My mother called to ask her father for some financial help to get us settled, and he said he would only help if she promised to allow me to be placed somewhere that possibly could give me some help. That's when I came to Childhelp Village in Virginia. If that hadn't worked, I probably would have been locked up in a juvenile facility before too long.

One of the first things I remember thinking shortly after I went to the Village was that there were children there who seemed just like me. I finally had someone to hang out with. For the first time, I fit in somewhere. And that made a huge difference in helping to eliminate the feeling of being different and all alone. Another thing I liked was having a routine of living—something constant and consistent. What might have been scary for someone else felt sort of comfortable to me.

For some reason, the people who worked in these villages seemed to really care, and so they would take time with you. They would ask you if you wanted to do this or that, not *tell* you to do something. A plan was created for us, and the staff took a lot of time explaining what it was we were trying to accomplish together. No one outside the Village had *ever* explained anything to me before.

Another thing that was really neat was that soon after anyone arrived, you were taken and allowed to pick out a brand new bicycle—one that was just to be yours and no one else's. I hadn't had much that was ever just mine, let alone a new bicycle. They had a group there called "Wheel Friends" that would help get the bikes and then come and take care of the repairs and maintenance, making sure they were in good running order. They were a great group. Even school was fun. Of course, we had chores, and we would get an allowance each week. We were also taught about how to be smart with our money.

My favorite thing at the Village was to work with the

animals. The Village is a beautiful place to call "home" with lots of land to roam. After being there for about a year, I was allowed to have certain animals that I took care of on my own. I fed them, cleaned their stalls, and basically did anything that was needed for their upkeep. For that, I got to have a lot of extra riding privileges. I love riding. The horses and I seemed to understand each other a lot. And I liked it that when I would go, my horse would see me, and come running up to me. I liked doing the chores there because it made me proud, and I felt appreciated for the first time.

Eventually, I got to take some of the new boys down to show them the animals for the first time after their arrival. That made me feel important and showed me that the people at the Village trusted me. We would get points added to our personal plans when we followed through on our assignments or chores, but it wasn't long before I would have done them whether I got points or not. I see now that it was a good lesson in learning to be responsible. It was also comforting for me to have some routine to follow since most of the time I had a hard time concentrating. We all had to go to therapy sessions, which I didn't mind. That's where I eventually found out about my ADD. There was also an art room where you could go and make things. That lady was really nice.

I really got to bring my reading and learning up a lot while at Childhelp. So, I am very grateful I was able to go there. They gave me another chance. The people there really care about what they do and the children. It turned my life around.

We all had a person who came from the outside to be our "Special Friend" for parties and to do activities. Mine was an admiral with lots of stars on his lapel, Admiral William Owens, who was the assistant to the head of the Joint Chiefs of Staff. He had lots of "pull" all over the Navy, and I really grew to like him. He's actually the person who gave me my first bike. That was the first day I met him.

Admiral Owens asked one day if I would like to go visit a submarine. He told me about a group that the Navy had created for young boys. They would meet and do things with the adult Navy guys and have uniforms and learn about life being a seaman. It wasn't long before I joined them and would go on outings once a month. It was fun and when I would come back, they let me tell about it sometimes in chapel on Sundays or in the cottages in the evening. I would show pictures we had taken and share what we did. The other children seemed to like that, and some of the guys would want to hang out with me because the Admiral arranged such neat things. He often allowed me to ask a group of friends to join us.

Finally when I turned 13, it was time to move on. Childhelp can't really keep the children after that age. Even though my mom was doing much better with her life and my brother and sister seemed happy, it was decided that I would be better off living elsewhere. My grandfather talked to my uncle and aunt who had retired and were living in California. They agreed to let me come and live with them in an effort to keep the family together. They lived in the Inland Valley and had some land they owned and were jointly farming with my grandfather. As it turned out, I loved it there. We had some animals on the farm, and so it was a familiar and happy atmosphere for me.

I am now almost 21 years old and have been enlisted with the Marine Corps for a little over a year. A lot of that is due to the positive influence of the Admiral being my Special Friend. I am stationed in San Diego. I keep in regular touch with the Admiral who has retired there, and we actually get together for dinner every time I am in town on leave. I go out to Childhelp Village in Beaumont, California every chance I get to visit and see the children. I made it, and I want them to know they can also. I hope I can be an inspiration to them—even if to just one of them.

My mom is doing well and has remarried. My sister is with the Marine Corps stationed in Tennessee. We talk often. My brother is in college and volunteers at a homeless shelter. He loves doing that and wants to do something where he helps less fortunate children. I have a girlfriend now, and we are thinking about getting married in a few years. But we are not going to rush things. I would like to have a couple of children of my own someday. I have a strong sense of faith that I learned from being at Childhelp. Things have turned out pretty well.

At one of the parties I attended for Childhelp Village in Beaumont, I got to thank Sara and Yvonne personally. That felt good. I had seen them when I was at the Village in Virginia but never really spoke with them much because I was too shy. It was great to thank them for "being there" for me through what they had created. It saved my life, I believe. At first, I thought I might want to go back and work for one of the Villages and with them. It was such a happy time in my life. But right now, I am getting to see so much more than I realized was out there in the world by being with the Marine Corps that I am not sure what I will eventually do. I have also thought that I might want to become a farmer, like my grandfather and uncle, and eventually take over the family farm. We have over 2,000 acres in California. Recently, I've been thinking that I might go to that oceanography school in San Diego when my enlistment is up. That, too, has caught my interest. The reality is that with the life I have now—anything is possible.

So, there it is. I am just one of the many success stories of Childhelp USA. I am sure that by picking up this book, you will come to know why it has been, and continues to be, an important presence for many lives over the years.

Sara and Yvonne—I hope your lives have turned out to be as blessed as mine has become. Thank you!

here i go...
ready or not!

RUBEN WALKS TOWARD VICTORY

*R*uben's eyes appeared to glaze over and didn't blink. "She will be mad at me," he said almost in a whisper, "and she won't talk to me when I grow up. I won't have brothers and sisters either—they'll be in jail. *Mammi* might use drugs if she gets upset, and then I'll have no mom."

His mom was the one person in this world Ruben knew best, and he had just confronted the fact that he could not rely on her. She sleeps beside the man who beats Ruben—the man she has chosen over him, his brothers, and sisters. She calls and promises Sunday visits, and then doesn't show up. The disappointment sends Ruben's built-up anticipation spiraling down into despair.

The under-sized boy retreated further into the over-stuffed chair, furrowed his brow, and looked down at the tiled floor. I recognized the signs of fear and saw Ruben falling further into a tornado of confusion and despair. He so longed to hear his mother say just once: *I'll love you no matter what.*

I sat on a chair across from a ten-year-old attempting to work his way through a personal crisis.

"Are you okay, Ruben?" I asked, seeing he was still someplace else.

Ruben gazed through my office floor-to-ceiling window where a warm autumn sun was sliding below a pastel horizon. Outside he could see birds flying, and squirrels and rabbits running through the nearby fields.

A phone rang in an adjoining office. His whole body jerked.

Ruben had been at a Childhelp Village now for two years. He came there almost drowning in anger—an anger born of longing for an unreliable mother who never made time to participate in the process of reclaiming her son. I had explained many times to her this was why Ruben could not go home from Childhelp to visit.

"By scheduling to visit and then not showing up, he doesn't trust you," I told her in awkward Spanish.

It was an ongoing dance of: "Yes, I'll be there,"—and sometimes she would—but often she would say, "Something has come up and I can't make it," and that's more or less how things had remained up until this particular Friday morning. Frozen in place. Then, for no apparent reason, Ruben intercepted me next to the auditorium bleachers during an awards assembly. For the first time in over a year, he had won for the "Most Improved." He had quickly blurted out something so fast I didn't understand what he was saying.

"You want to do what?" I had to ask him to speak again. I smiled reflexively, accustomed to Ruben's excited ramblings immediately preceding an anticipated visit from his mom. Ruben looked serious. He lived for his mother and cared for nothing except this troubled woman who would not keep her son safe enough to retain custody.

"I don't want my mom to come for a visit this weekend," Ruben repeated, "because when she leaves, I get too upset and mess up."

I nodded and replied, "Really?"

That had been one of Ruben's ongoing issues—how he acted after a visit from his mother.

"She's scheduled for this Sunday, so someone will have to tell her to come another weekend," I said to Ruben in response.

Ruben's face reddened like he'd just been slapped on both cheeks.

"Who do you want to tell her, Ruben?"

"You."

"Okay."

He nodded emphatically, and then walked away.

I shook my head in amazement.

In all the months I had worked with Ruben, he'd shown zero interest in himself, his therapy, his program, or his coping skills. In fact, he seemed to care only about two things: being cool and spending more time with "*Mammi.*"

The awards assembly ended with all 80 Childhelp children in the Village promising to focus on the character trait "responsibility" the next month. My ten boys and myself returned to the cottage up the hill that was theirs, where dinner and an after-dinner quiet time awaited. I reminded myself that I had promised to deliver a message to Ruben's mother but was immediately distracted when a group of the boys descended on me with a myriad of favor requests, attention-getting behaviors, and bids for praise. I soon found myself totally absorbed by "my family"—so much so that by dinnertime, I had stored my concerns about Ruben on a quiet shelf in the back closet of my mind.

A ringing phone jolted me from my disjointed thoughts. Grace before dinner had just concluded and hot food was making its journey down the long table, boy-to-boy, hand-to-hand. One of the caregivers, Maria, picked up the phone.

"It's Ruben's mother, and she wants to confirm her visit for Sunday," the social worker mouthed to me, covering the mouthpiece.

"I'll call her back after dinner. We're eating now."

Maria delivered the message in Spanish, and then hung up.

I had just served myself when the phone behind me rang again. I got up and answered this time. No sense ruining everyone else's dinner.

"*Hola. ¿Puedo hablar con mi niño, Ruben?*" (May I speak to my son, Ruben?)

"*Sí. Sí claro* (Yes, of course.)," I smiled nervously; the moment of truth was at hand.

Suddenly Ruben was standing beside me, studying me. I could tell by his pale lips and flexing cheek muscles that he knew it was his mother. He stood barely over four feet with a frail build and thick black hair. He had dark skin—Native Plains Indian coloring. I remembered that just a few months ago, this same boy had dressed in gang-banger outfits—strutting, gesturing, and spewing defiance.

"Don't worry," I assured him with my hand over the mouthpiece. "I'll tell her you don't want to see her this Sunday. You don't have to tell her anything."

He shrugged. "It's okay. I'll tell her." He nodded with head and shoulders suddenly thrown back—an emphatic gesture of confidence.

"Are you sure? You don't have to. Maria can translate for me if you want."

He drew in a deep breath, rocked on his heel, and eyed the phone.

"No, that's okay," he asserted, half smiling.

How did this boy who had specialized in brat punk-hood for the past year grow up without my noticing? The boy rounded his shoulders and took the phone.

"¿*Mammi?*" His voice changed to that of a two-year-old. I thought he might not be able to speak his mind.

"Wait!" I said and motioned for Maria to listen in on the extension. "Be ready!"

The social worker picked up the other phone in the kitchen and walked up beside Ruben—the two of us stood on either side, twin towers of support.

Ruben continued. "*No quiero que vengas este Domingo.* (I don't want you to come this Sunday.) *No puedo funcionar despuès de las visitas.* (I can't function after your visits.) *Tengo que deportar bien.* (I have to be good.)"

There was a silence for a moment on the other end of the phone, and then she unleashed a blast of cursing at her young son.

Ruben listened quietly. When his mother finally took a breath, he finished his thought: "*Este Domingo no, pero el próximo.*" (Not this Sunday, the next.) He then handed the receiver to me and stood frozen as I said goodbye to his mother and hung up the phone.

Ruben's eyes became heavy and filled with tears.

"I have upset *Mammi*," he fretted.

"Ruben, you've been sad so many times when she *didn't* show up." My voice was gentle and I tried to wrap the truth in pretty paper. "It's not just your problem to be sad about. It's hers, too. Maybe she'll have to cry, too."

He wiped his eyes.

I stopped and noted we were on the razor sharp turning point of an adult decision taken by a child growing up in the space of a day.

"Your mother loves you, always will, and she'll always be your mother. She might be hurt right now, but it will be okay."

He looked uncertain.

"Your feelings hurt a lot, missing her, wondering why

she picked that man instead of just making a home for you."

He looked into my eyes for several moments before finally nodding.

"But you always loved her. No matter what."

He had to digest that statement before nodding again.

"And so for her, too. She'll love you, no matter what."

He just looked back at me, eyes hooded with inward thoughts. In truth he knew his mother's love was permanent—that was not the question.

"You wanted to make a change, and you were honest with yourself, and knew that you needed space from your mom."

No reaction, just a stare.

"*You* stood up for yourself tonight because you said, 'Time out, Mom. I love you, but I need a break.' You gave yourself a great gift, and now no one can take that away. You have *yourself!*"

I waited, watching for Ruben's reaction.

"I did the right thing, and I have myself?"

He rolled the words over his tongue like a lapidary polishing stones, studied me, and then glanced in the direction of one brick wall, which held a phrase written on a bulletin board. "*I'll always love you, it's your behavior we're talking about.*"

"Yes, Ruben, and I am so very proud of you."

I felt tears streaming down my cheeks at this point, unable to hold them back any longer.

Ruben looked at me full on—incredulous. He said nothing for a full ten seconds, mouth ajar, and then the first smile since he'd arrived tonight.

"I never saw anyone cry for me." And then suddenly a grin broke that spread ear-to-ear.

"You know what? I can do this," he whispered. "God has faith in me."

Silence filled the room while he looked once again at the bulletin board. I didn't know what to expect—he was suddenly talking about God. That was an idea he seemed uncomfortable with as recently as two months ago, and now he was referring to God as if they were old friends. And then I noticed a twinkle in his eye and the makings of another grin as if he had suddenly uncovered a great secret.

"Okay, God, here I am," he announced as he raised his chin and threw his shoulders back.

Ruben took a deep breath while he saw the reflection of himself in the tall window of the room framed against the darkness outside.

As a smile spread across his face, he turned and looked me directly in the eyes, and proceeded to say, "Here I go . . . ready or not."

And marched down the hallway to his room.

I stood for a moment taking in what I had just seen, and then collapsed into a chair in tears. I think we just had another miracle.

I chose this career in children's therapy because I wanted to make a difference in young lives at a time when they needed help the most—those formative years just before the teens. Once I came to work at Childhelp Village, I quickly realized God had blessed me with an opportunity to be a guide for these children's healing. But like Anna in the *King and I,* I was unprepared for how much I would learn from those I sought to teach.

Ready, set, go.

Kel and Anne Geddes at the Humanitarian
Awards Luncheon in Los Angeles, California (2002).

Ribbon-cutting at the grand opening of Childhelp
Children's Center of Arizona (1998). (Left to right)
Molly Beeson, Carol Lawrence, Rhonda Fleming, Sara,
Mary Hart, Jane Seymour, Collin Raye, Yvonne, Ralna English.

Merv Griffin presenting the deed to
his dude ranch to Sara and Yvonne
to establish the Childhelp USA
Merv Griffin Village of Arizona.

Yvonne, Julie Wrigley, and Sara
at National Charity Awards,
Washington D.C. (2001).

2002 Humanitarian Awards Luncheon in Los Angeles,
California. Honorees pictured with founders: Lynne Cheney,
Woman of the World; Phil Morris, Heart of Compassion
Award; and Anne and Kel Geddes, Angel Award.

CHAPTER ELEVEN

the miracles continue

EMBRACING AN ATTITUDE OF GRATITUDE

*I*n 1996, Yvonne and I, along with our husbands, were definitely guided to move from the Los Angeles area to Scottsdale, Arizona. We had long been drawn to this wonderful area and decided to relocate the national headquarters there.

It wasn't long after our relocation that we began to search for a place in the area of our new home to build another very much needed residential treatment village. We knew we could never be too far from our work and our mission. Our daily involvement with the children, whom we refer to as our "treasures," had long become a way of life, and we weren't willing to ever lose our direct connection. Once again, we found ourselves committed to finding just the right location and property around the Phoenix/Scottsdale area.

We had been looking at different properties—property to buy, and property various people had offered as a donation on which to build a village—and nothing really seemed exactly right. As we were on our search, we stumbled onto an area located about 70 miles outside Phoenix called Wickenburg. We felt this area would be perfect for the children because of the open air and beautiful environment that surrounded it. It had a park and thousands of acres that were undeveloped. It appeared to be a perfect setting and our hearts told us this was the area where we should go. My husband, Bob Sigholtz, was a friend of Johnny Gardner, who was a close friend of Merv Griffin, who had a lot of acreage in Wickenburg. Johnny had promised to contact Mr. Griffin to see if he might help us. However, he passed away before he was able to do so. I had an indelible dream after that which stated we were to have our Village in Wickenburg.

One day we mentioned writing a letter to introduce ourselves to Mr. Griffin and express our need for a Village and that we were very interested in the Wickenburg area. Although Mr. Griffin had attended some fund raising events in Los Angeles years ago, he did not really know us that well personally.

Before we mailed the letter, a lady who was working for us at the time said, "Well, I know a contact of Mr. Griffin's. Perhaps we could go through him." She and her family had spent the last Thanksgiving at the five-star Merv Griffin's Wickenburg Inn and Dude Ranch in Wickenburg. She said that while they were there, she had met and struck up a conversation with a man who was in a leadership role with GrifWick, Mr. Griffin's national company. We wrote the letter with the hopes that through the connection, we could somehow reach Mr. Griffin directly without having to go through the many "chains of command."

To our great joy, we were contacted soon after by an associate, Larry Cohen, President of GrifWick. He said this just might be something that would be of interest to Mr.

Griffin. During conversations that followed, we found out that Mr. Griffin did not own the 2,000 acres of additional land, as we had thought, but he did own the dude ranch. At first we were a bit disappointed because our proposal was asking for property to build the Village. We were encouraged not to give up and allowed him to present our proposal to Mr. Griffin anyway. It might just be that he would have some thoughts about how to help us with securing something in that area for the Village.

As it turned out, he decided this *was* something he would be interested in supporting. He asked his attorneys to check Childhelp USA out—to first see how financially sound we were and what it was that our organization was doing. He sent one of his attorneys, Kim Sinatra, to see our Village in Beaumont, California. Afterward, the attorney talked to us at great lengths on the phone. She fell in love with the Village and felt that it was something to which Mr. Griffin's heart would really respond. She went back to him and told some stories of the different children and what she had seen. She explained that she was most impressed with the quality of care that we were giving the children and the in-depth detail that was adhered to for their individual issues and care—the environment we created for them and how she was fascinated by all the different programs that we offered. She particularly pointed out how 91 cents out of every dollar spent reached the children.

With these glowing reports, a flame was ignited within him to do something—to be a part of our project. As our interaction blossomed, it was made clear to us that Mr. Griffin wanted us to take a look at his dude ranch as a possible venue for the Village. We were swept with excitement. We had just merely been trying to acquire an ally to find some land—but he was suggesting we might consider his dude ranch. Once again, God's underlying energy and our mission had become infectious. We went out to see the dude ranch and knew right off that it would just be a perfect setting for the children. It was a very healing environment.

Efforts were already underway for our "Spirit of the Children" gala in October of 2000 to raise funding for our Arizona project organized by our Arizona State Board of Directors and Phoenix Chapter. We knew we were going forward with this, our next Childhelp Village residential treatment center. And we were going to do whatever it took. We were elated when Mr. Griffin accepted our invitation to attend the gala. That evening, as a surprise to all in attendance, he announced that he was donating the deed to his acclaimed Merv Griffin Wickenburg Inn and Dude Ranch for our use complete with furnishings, horses—the whole works. Again, another of God's miracles!

But that's not all.

Inspired by this wonderful land donation given by Merv Griffin, we had a generous gift from Julie Wrigley of $2.5 million soon afterward. We were on our way to another dream being realized. Along with great additional assistance and support, the Childhelp USA Merv Griffin Village of Arizona opened in June 2002.

Merv stated at the gala and many times since that donating this ranch was the most rewarding thing that he has ever done. He would go on to say, "At Childhelp USA's Merv Griffin Village of Arizona, I know the children will begin to heal in the wonderful ranch environment and with the guidance of the dedicated staff. When I heard the tragic stories about how many severely abused children who, without treatment, turn into emotionally disturbed adults, I knew I had an important and perfect property to give." We knew from our own blessings from helping these children that truly, *his* rewards had just begun. And he has visited the Village interfacing with the children—who just love him.

This Village is expected to become a national showcase that will serve as a model for treating severely abused children. Also, in our future planning, there is to be an International Training Center located in Arizona. It will effectively spread knowledge through training workshops and presentations of research findings to child abuse professionals throughout the world. We feel ongoing gratitude for Merv. He has become one of our extraordinary *earthly angels*. Thank you, Merv!

We cherish the relationships we are building everyday with the wonderful people who step forward in support of our Arizona children, particularly those who stepped forward to make it happen beyond belief—Carol and Jim Hebets, Linda and Bill Pope, Sharon and Michael Lechter, Diane and Bruce Halle, Chuck Theisen, and Julie Wrigley. We could never have come to where we are if we hadn't had God send these and other precious *earthly angels*. Thanks to you and all our volunteers from the bottom of our hearts.

One of the greatest creations over the past few years has sprung out of Dick Willey's initial concept of creating advocacy centers and mobile advocacy units. In Phoenix, we have been able to co-create a magnificent center with the help of a wonderful man, Russell "Russ" Huber, a retired child abuse detective. It opened in 1998 and is named after a major donor, James Archer. It expands on the same outline that the Willey's created in Tennessee, and we have been able to use it to train others worldwide. Certainly, accolades go to *all* our volunteers and donors who have helped to make this happen.

It is amazing how Russ and the staff have managed to bring together and craft a harmonious co-existence among all those who participate in the programs here under one roof—forensic interviewers, detectives, Child Protective Services caseworkers, police, psychologists, mental health therapists, doctors, prosecutors, our own staff, interns, and volunteers. It is truly remarkable. This increased communication among agencies helps all those involved in understanding their roles and their case needs. This also enables quicker prosecutions through more efficient case processing and keeps the child's trauma to a minimum: one facility where all can be done—and quite often done at one time. We do provide follow up and ongoing therapy for the child.

The moment anyone enters—especially the children—he or she can feel the peaceful and safe atmosphere that permeates the interior spreading outward. There are individual investigation interview rooms that are designed from a concept we created wherein the child can feel safe and is encouraged to tell his or her story from their own perspective. This way, the child can convey to the interviewer what happened to them in their own words and descriptions. There is even a beautiful meditation room donated by Rhonda Fleming off the lobby that gives respite to the family members and staff in times when one needs to step away for silence and centering. Dealing with child abuse is not an easy journey for anyone.

Phoenix has become our flagship Advocacy Center. We have been able to train all walks of professionals who come in contact with child abuse, and that includes teachers, emergency room doctors, and school nurses. We have even had delegations tour us from Australia, Canada, Japan, Russia, and France, and show interest in creating centers in their countries. The Center utilizes a highly effective, one-stop approach to the investigation and treatment of child abuse. The child-friendly environment and team approach increases efficiency while minimizing the trauma to the child. Six thousand one hundred children, including siblings and therapy clients, received services in the last calendar year. We are also working with Native American communities in Northern Arizona. We just had our Mobile Advocacy Unit under-written, so it will be operating and traveling to those areas soon.

Sometimes it takes our breath away when we think about how we as two young girls, who started out on this mission so many years ago in Japan by "happenstance," now have almost 2,000 volunteers nationwide with chapters and auxiliaries in California, Tennessee, Arizona, Maryland, Virginia, Michigan, and Washington, D.C. They have worked tirelessly to make Childhelp USA successful in helping over 3,000,000 children since its inception. We also have the support of some of the kindest and well-known celebrities who all deserve Academy Awards for their tireless participation.

Today there continues to be more wonderful things unfolding all the time—miracles and magical moments like those that have appeared all throughout our mission, from the first moment we embraced this voyage around helping children. That's really the thread that consistently runs through our story—the miracles that take place even with the challenges.

With the opening of our latest Village in Arizona and the inauguration of our national headquarters, we have once again come to a place of gratitude for all that happens every time we step out to be the voice for a helpless child—every time we break the silence about these children. We have been blessed to have my husband, Bob Sigholtz, and Yvonne's late husband, Don Fedderson, support us over the years—as has my son, John Hopkins. It also is with great pride that we have my daughter-in-law, Sylvia Hopkins, and Yvonne's daughter, Dionne Fedderson Archer, working along side of us these days. They will one day become our successors.

a special friend's memories

SOMEONE I WILL NEVER FORGET

Although I've toured the residential village numerous times over the years, each time I become a Special Friend to one of the children, I like to spend my first visit on campus allowing the child to give me a tour of the facility that is now "home." The children are so proud of where they live and under the guise of being my "tour guide"—the beauty of the child comes through in his or her words and descriptions. In this way, I can gain some instant insight into their world and get a sense of who they are as I am led through the Village.

One of my particular Special Friends was a boy I will never forget. Tommy was one of the cutest six-year-old boys I've ever seen—blond crew cut, freckles on his face, and a big smile with one front tooth missing. Not only was he cute—he was sweet and very easy to love. He was allowed only supervised visits with his father; his mother had abandoned him.

I remember the first day we met. Tommy took my hand and we chatted nonstop as we started "the tour." While we were walking down the steps from the Administration Building, a little red car pulled into a parking space, Tommy shouted, "Dad!" and went running toward the man getting out. There were hugs from both father and an accompanying older woman (Tommy's grandmother—his dad's mom), and I wasn't quite sure what to do. So, I just stayed close and stood watching. I believe they assumed I was a Village employee since there were no introductions. That was perfectly fine with me. One look at Tommy's father and Ray Bradbury's *The Illustrated Man* came to mind. This man had tattoos on every visible part of his body.

After a few minutes, the father and grandmother went into the Administration Building. Tommy and I continued our tour, walking toward the village ranch. We stopped for a few minutes, and Tommy pulled some grass and tried to feed one of the miniature horses that was not at all interested in his offering. He talked to the little horse and eventually said, "You look sad today. Maybe your mommie left you, too." A light bulb went on in my head, and I caught myself thinking that he was revealing a part of himself.

The following day, I spoke with the head clinician at the Village and learned that Tommy's mother had, indeed, abandoned him. I also learned his father was a heroin addict and a tattoo artist by profession. He was very affectionate with Tommy and seemed to love him. But to borrow a phrase from one of the other Village children I heard more that once: "He loved drugs more than me."

Tommy did well at the Village and was in residence for only about six months. Over that time, we did have several fun visits and shared one very memorable Christmas together. My heart was broken when he went to a foster home. But I knew this also meant that he was making progress, and I trusted that he was happy and thriving. I think of him often with that big-tooth-missing smile.

I received a call from the Volunteer Director of the Village a couple of weeks after Tommy left.

She said, "Loretta, I know you're mourning Tommy's departure. But Carson in 4B really needs a Special Friend. Won't you consider him?"

Tommy had also been in 4B. Therefore, I had met and connected briefly with Carson on a number of occasions and knew him as a lovely, neat child. I signed on right away.

I have been with Carson almost six years now, and my family and I have taken many excursions to play in the snow, shop for school supplies or clothing, gone out to movies, play games at an arcade, and have lunch and/or dinner. One of the best events of all was when we spent a day at Disney's California Adventure. Neither Carson, my husband, daughter, nor I had been there previously, so that was a big treat. Carson and my daughter got soaked on a water ride that my husband and I declined to get on. We ate hot dogs, pizza, ice cream, and other junk food for the day. We loved being there and being together.

On shopping trips, Carson often asked if he could buy a gift for someone else—usually a staff person. Once, he went on a campaign to "spruce up" the Village. And I remember the day he asked if we could buy a plant. He even knew the driving directions to the nursery. I had expected him to want a toy on our shopping outing that day. But when we got to the nursery, he chose a rose called "little sizzler." We planted it near his cottage, but it began to look very sad after just a couple of weeks because of the sandy soil. Carson and I agreed we would try to save it by bringing it to my home and putting it in my yard. I would tend it for him, and he could visit to help care for it. It flourishes today, and we have named it "Carson's Rose."

Another time, Carson was in the hospital suffering from pneumonia, and I went to visit. He was sleeping when I walked into his room. Although tall for a 10-year-old, as I gazed upon him curled up in the bed, he looked small and vulnerable. I had brought balloons and proceeded to tie them to the end of his bed. After which, I pulled out his favorite book, *The Velveteen Rabbit*, and read to him until he fell asleep. He slept for some time and when awakened by a noise outside his door, he opened his eyes, took a few seconds to focus on me, and said, "Oh, I've been missing you."

Carson loves my daughter, and she loves him, too. Carson's bond with her is surprisingly strong. He is always happy when connected to her doing things together. When my daughter comes with me on a visit, she brings him gifts. He loves the surprises. She also sends him cards on all occasions, has helped him make a scrapbook of our times together, has helped with his homework, and has taught him why double negatives are a "no-no." They are wonderful together. Carson is smart, fun to be with, eager, quick to learn, curious, and very creative.

We have celebrated each of Carson's birthdays and Christmases during the years as Special Friends. We have created a close relationship that feels very much like family. In the years I've known Carson, he only had one or two visits from an aunt and then she just vanished. He has had no contact with his parents. My husband, daughter, and I have been the only constants in his life outside the Village for six years—over half his lifetime. He counts on us and we seem to be the only family he knows. Sometimes, "on accident," he calls me "Mom."

As we drove him home after our last excursion, Carson blurted out something horrible that his father had done to him. This was not the first time he had been so forthcoming, and it's wonderful to know he feels secure enough to share that part of his past with us. We all know that breaking the silence about what happened is the beginning toward healing. He is beginning to understand that none of it was his fault.

We love Carson and are grateful to be his Special Friends.

sharing the gift of healing

A CHILD ABUSE SURVIVOR GIVES BACK

*O*ne bright sunny October day in 1969, my sister and I were peacefully playing records in the bedroom we shared in my grandmother's house. We felt safe for the first time in a long while. My mother had recently taken us and fled in the night from the abusive circumstances we had endured while living with my stepfather. Ralph, the stepfather, had done more to injure my body and spirit than I had let anyone know about at that time. It went without saying: I was more than glad to be away from him.

Mom had just finished getting dressed up for a job interview and came in to say goodbye. We stopped briefly to give her a hug, and she was out the door. Our focus quickly returned to the record playing.

Suddenly, we were interrupted by a neighborhood boy's shouts as he was entering the house: "Your mother's been shot! A big man in a white car!"

I knew immediately it was Ralph.

As I ran to look out the window, I saw my mom lying on

the sidewalk. She was bleeding from around her shoulder. I quickly called the police, telling them where we were, what had just happened, giving them a full description of Ralph, his car, and our previous address so they could locate him. I then ran outside to join my sister and grandmother, who were screaming hysterically, to discover my mom lying unconscious on the ground. Before I knew it, a neighbor from across the street had grabbed us and ushered us back into the safe confines of the house.

As I sat in the living room amidst a frenzy of police, para-medics, and neighbors, with tears running down my face, I just kept praying that God would not take my mother from me. I felt tremendous guilt, shame, and fear. I sat thinking to myself: *Maybe if I had been better, this would not have happened.* Somehow in my young mind I thought I had something to do with what had just occurred and that I was a "bad girl." When word came that my mother died, I was left numb and empty. I felt exhausted and cold inside.

Many people feared Ralph as much as I had. There had actually been witnesses to a threat the night before the shooting. I was engulfed with so much fear of this man that I did not tell anyone of the severe beatings, sexual and mental abuse I had endured by him. Ralph was sentenced to involuntary manslaughter and given five years.

Even after his conviction and incarceration, I lived in fear of this man everyday. And it would eventually prove to be not without merit. Ralph ultimately received a parole and was released. One day while in high school, I spied Ralph in his car, and he proceeded to follow me as I walked home. I told a friend who helped me go to the police to give a depo-sition. Ralph's parole was revoked. Having this knowledge, I still lived in fear of him coming after me. I would often wear the metal pop can lids on my knuckles when alone in prepa-ration to fight for my life. I was in constant fear that if he got out, he would come to find me. As the years passed by, a gnawing hatred built up inside me.

I grew up, married twice, and had children of my own. After the second failed marriage, I sought the professional help of a counselor. I felt I couldn't go on blinded by fear and hatred. My spirit was dying inside. I was truly blessed with a wonderful woman counselor who would ultimately guide me into a path of healing that would restore my faith *and* connection with God. I prayed often over the anger I still had and the hatred toward Ralph and what he had done to my family and me. On July 4, 1993, I walked into a church for the first time in years. It was there that my recovery began to take on a rapid change.

The following year, I attended a singles retreat in the mountains of Arizona. Something started to stir within me. I knew that as long as I held on to the pain and hatred, I would always remain a victim. I knew I must find a way to move into forgiveness for what had been done. As I stood before the group sharing my story and desire for healing, I started to cry and my body began to shake. It felt like the floodgates had suddenly been flung open and all the years of pain and fear were pouring out of me. By the time the weekend was over, I felt renewed and a sense of freedom for the first time in years.

About that time, I met a new friend, Ralna. We were both single mothers. We shared a lot together about our past. When Ralna found out about what I had been through, she said she wanted to introduce me to an organization that had become an important part of her life. That would turn out to be Childhelp USA. I went to a luncheon with her and found out that I could possibly help other abused and neglected children. I decided to give it a try, and it has been my miracle tonic.

That was some years ago. Today, rather than dwell on my past and make excuses, I have chosen to use the gift of survival that was given to me to help others. I knew somewhere inside me that God had directed me here. *There are no coincidences.* I have come to realize that by involving ourselves with the children in our communities who are in need, we can do much to avoid the broken families, violence, and pain that is carried by so many of the generations of today. It has also brought great healing to my own life.

I became a member of the Greater Phoenix Chapter of Childhelp USA about eight years ago. I have also become a Special Friend. I had one young boy who was reunited with his family. That was wonderful. My second "friend" has been with me for about seven years now. I have seen this young boy, who wouldn't respond or hardly speak in the beginning, grow into a bright, cheerful boy. My Special Friend, Dennis, gave me the best Christmas present in 2002 when I visited him in California. For the first time ever, he reached out to me for a hug when I was ready to leave. Dennis had been diagnosed with severe abuse and was also somewhat autistic. This was a monumental step for him. I was thrilled! He has now started to read and do math. This, I truly believe, would not have happened if he had not experienced the love, care, and kindness found at the Childhelp USA residential treatment facility.

I was given the gift to survive, which has ultimately sparked within a desire to help others understand the tragedy of abuse in a child's life. As a volunteer at the Childhelp Children's Center of Phoenix, I have been able to share that gift.

One day there was a young teen girl in for an investigation on the suspicion she had been abused. As I watched her diligently trying to do homework, I knew by instinct that this beautiful young girl was trying to hide some deep fear and pain. She kept her eyes down and constantly pulled her dark hair down to cover her face. Although we have been trained to recognize certain signs of withdrawal that signify abuse, I felt I knew this girl's personal pain all too well.

I stepped over to her and quietly said, "You don't have to do your homework now if you don't want to. Your teacher will understand. If you need anything, I am here. Even if you just need a shoulder to cry on."

In the next instant, she was sobbing in my arms. I told her that it was okay to cry, and she would be safe. After what seemed like an eternity, she was later able to open up to the detective. And the process had begun to protect this darling soul.

I continue to be a Special Friend to Dennis and to participate in Childhelp activities. This has ignited what looks to be a lifelong passion of working with these children. Today, both my beautiful daughters have become volunteers at Childhelp. Childhelp USA has become a second family of nurturing for us, and I continue to receive much more than I give. Each day I thank God that I am alive and well and able to use my life to help others who have known abuse. As a mother, and for the love of a child, I am here to stay as long as I can be of service.

Thank you, Sara and Yvonne, for what you have created.

epilogue

*T*he stories of the lives of the children from Japan and Vietnam we helped save, as well as the children over the years in the United States, continue to this day. Many have now grown to become successful adults. We hear about them, like Loan, from time to time. Each time we do, we cry for joy. They are our blessings. And we will never get over the sorrow of the ones we've lost.

We laugh as we remember those two girls preparing a speech to decline graciously taking on another project for these special children. It was not in our plan, yet we now know it was certainly part of God's plan for us. The organization of Childhelp USA begins each day knowing that our efforts will touch the life of a child in need. Childhelp USA has become the very essence of our mission and our reason for being.

We have been extraordinarily blessed by this journey we have undertaken—by the children we serve, by the volunteers, by our incredible staff, by our families, and by our friends. Some have shared their stories with you in this book.

I must say I don't know how we could have done all this without the tireless effort and commitment of the dedicated individuals in our chapters and auxiliaries across the country who have been our pillars since the beginning. They are angels of the greatest magnitude and bright light. Through times of difficulty, they have been there to support us in any way that has been needed. We have a tremendous place of love for them in our hearts. They are the inspiration behind a great number of the special events. Their value cannot be measured. We are especially thankful for Efrem Zimbalist, Jr. and John Stamos, two of our Celebrity Ambassadors, who continue to return year after year to make our Christmas pageant and party at Village West a heart-warming success. The children love them.

It gives us a smile and a laugh when we remember our first event in Japan all those years ago as assistants in a magic show to raise money for our first 11 orphans. (But that's a story for our next book.) We've come a long way. We give thanks for it all. We are in awe of what has happened. But most of all, we are extremely grateful for the presence of God in all areas of our operations and the miracles that keep happening along the way.

When we had nearly finished building the first Childhelp Village in Beaumont, California, one of the last structures to go up on the property was the Rhonda Fleming Chapel. Children were already staying at the Village, and the chapel's foundation had just been laid. We were at the Village one afternoon to observe the beginning of the chapel's construction when a young boy came rushing up to us, all excited, with a big smile on his face.

"Guess what, guess what? They're building a house for God," he gushingly announced, "*and* He's gonna live right next door to me!"

People sometimes want to know how we have gotten through it all. And we have even been met with: "Why do you care so much?" Our answer is that we love all our children, and their stories break our hearts wide open each time we hear another. How could we not care? It's difficult to bear when we see their precious, innocent faces, and we find out what has happened to them. But no matter how tough their lives were before coming to Childhelp, we know that they are in a safe place now, and we're doing everything possible to help them heal. We know for sure that every child who walks through our doors will find love.

We think about the children whom we haven't met yet, who are still in the throes of the horror of child abuse. Then we look at our children and take comfort in the fact that at least these children are warm and safe and on the road to recovery. And it's then we are reminded—*they're* the lucky ones.

Little did we realize as innocent young girls starting out in Japan to help some orphaned and abandoned children we found in the streets that we would be ultimately led to break the silence on a larger scale of abuse and neglect right here at home. After over 40 years of working for this cause, we have no doubt today about what mission God wanted us to pursue—and to continue to pursue.

We will continue to speak out and do everything we can—for as long as we can—to move these dear children from a loss of innocence to a world of healing and love.

Blessings,

Sara and Yvonne

Sara, Sylvia Hopkins (daughter-in-law), Yvonne, Carol Hebets
(Arizona Board Member), and Dionne Fedderson Archer
(Yvonne's daughter) at the Celebrity Fight Night VIP Reception (2003).

Yvonne, Muhammad
Ali, and Sara at the
Celebrity Fight Night
VIP Reception (2003).

The next generation:
Sylvia Hopkins and
Dionne Fedderson
Archer.

Our beloved husbands Bob Sigholtz
and the late Don Fedderson.

national day
of hope prayer

Dear God,

Our prayer is for the children, little ones so small,
Who suffer neglect, abuse, and pain behind a silent wall.
Please protect and comfort them;
Let Your presence calm their fear.
Give them courage to tell someone,
Help all of us to hear.

Instill in each one of us to remember them in our prayers.
Please give them hope and
Let them know a nation truly cares.
For the love of a child,
Amen.

Author and co-founder Sara O'Meara. Author and co-founder Yvonne Fedderson.

about the founders

Sara O'Meara—Chairman and CEO

Since 1959, Mrs. Sara O'Meara has provided leadership in humanitarian service to children throughout the world. As a Childhelp USA co-founder, Mrs. O'Meara is actively involved in the development and oversight of one of the oldest and largest national nonprofits dedicated to preventing and treating child abuse. The organization has put a national spotlight on the problem of child abuse in America and developed cutting-edge solutions.

As Chairman and CEO of Childhelp USA, Sara serves as the organization's key spokesperson and has primary responsibility for fund development and overall oversight of the organization's business. She has served on the boards of international organizations with child welfare. As a board member for the International Union of Child Welfare, she was the sole United States representative among First Ladies and ministers of numerous nations. Sara has received more than 50 awards for her service to children, including the Fraternal Order of Eagles Humanitarian award. Others include an award for international collaboration to prevent child abuse presented by the Queen of England; a U.S. Department of Justice award presented by President Ronald Reagan; and an award from the National Federation of Business and Professional Women's Clubs. She, like Mrs. Yvonne Fedderson, has been the recipient of several awards in Washington, D.C., including the National Caring Award and The Hubert Humphrey Memorial Award at the Touchdown Club, and the Lifetime Achievement Award at the National Charity Awards Dinner.

Mrs. Sara O'Meara was born Sara Buckner in Knoxville, Tennessee and was educated at Briarcliff Junior College, New York; Endicott College, Beverly, Massachusetts; The Sorbonne, France; and Pasadena Playhouse, California. Sara is married to Robert Sigholtz and makes her home in Paradise Valley, Arizona in close proximity to the National Headquarters for Childhelp USA. Sara has a son, John Hopkins. Her other son, Charles, was killed in 1988 in an auto accident. She also has a stepdaughter Taryn and three grandchildren.

Yvonne Fedderson—Co-founder and President

For more than four decades, Mrs. Yvonne Fedderson has devoted her life to helping children in need. As a Childhelp USA co-founder, Mrs. Fedderson is actively involved in the development and oversight of the nonprofit organization, along with Mrs. Sara O'Meara. As President, Mrs. Fedderson's focus is upon developing and supporting the organization's 20 chapters and auxiliaries. More than 1,800 volunteers nationwide organize fund-raising events in their communities, which produce more that $2 million annually.

Since 1994, Mrs. Fedderson has also served as President

and CEO of her late husband's company, Don Fedderson Productions. Her responsibilities involve managing the rights of the television programs he produced, including *Family Affair*, *My Three Sons*, and *The Betty White Show*. She has served on the company's board of directors for more than 30 years. Mrs. Fedderson, a graduate of the Pasadena Playhouse, under the name of Yvonne Lime, has had an extensive acting career in film, television, and stage.

Mrs. Fedderson has been active in a number of humanitarian organizations including the Assistance League, and the Mary and Joseph League, as well as several professional organizations. She has also served on the board of directors of Children to Children, Inc. and the International Alliance on Child Abuse and Neglect. Yvonne has received more than 45 honors and awards for her service to children, some of which include the National Children's Alliance's Champions of Children Award, the State of California Legislature's Woman of the World Award, and the Women's International Center's Living Legacy Award. She and Mrs. O'Meara have been given the Kiwanis World Service Medal, the American Ireland Fund Humanitarian Award, The University of California Riverside Chancellor's Founder's Award, and *Family Circle Magazine's* "Women Who Make a Difference."

Yvonne Lime Fedderson was born in Glendale, California and now makes her home in Paradise Valley, Arizona, which is near the National Headquarters for Childhelp USA. Her daughter Dionne Fedderson Archer also lives in Paradise Valley.

SILENCE*broken*

Additional Story Contributors

Dionne Fedderson Archer
Rev. Timothy Drom
Neil Frame
Rebecca Heller
Sylvia Hopkins
Cheryl Ladd
Dawn McCown
Chris Monaco, Ph.D.
Kaleb Powers
Jane Seymour
Marilee Walker
Betty White

Jean Patterson Bone
Lynn Elder
Darah Grimm
Pauline Hoopes
Russell Huber
Tran Thi Kim Loan
Maria Michel
Sandra Owen
Darlene Rich
Loretta Akana Sturla
Chuck Weber
Linda and Dick Willey

Celebrity Ambassadors

Susan Anton
The Bellamy Brothers
Pat Boone
Joyce Bulifant
Carol Connors
Norm Crosby
Phyllis Diller
Rhonda Fleming
David Foster
Leeza Gibbons
Melissa Gilbert
Lee Greenwood
Florence Henderson
David Keith
Carol Lawrence
Mary Ann Mobley
Nancy O'Dell

Molly Beeson
Clint Black and Lisa
  Hartman Black
Gary Collins
Mary Costa
John D'Aquino
Ralna English
Raymond Floyd
Glenn Frey
Kathie Lee Gifford
Amy Grant
Mary Hart
Anne Jeffreys
Cheryl Ladd
Ron Masak
Phil Morris
Jamie O'Neal

SILENCE*broken*

Merlin Olsen	Matthew Perry
Sasha Pieterse	Jimmy Pinchak
Collin Raye	Jack Scalia
Dr. Laura Schlessinger	Jane Seymour
T.G. Sheppard	John Stamos
Connie Stevens	Alan Thicke
Linda Thompson	Pam Tillis
Heather Tom	Kathleen Turner
Phil Vassar	Caitlin Wachs
Betty White	Barbara and Steve Young
Jack Youngblood	Efrem Zimbalist, Jr.

Thank you for helping us to teach these abused and neglected children their true worth.

In special recognition of Celebrity Fight Night and its founder Jimmy Walker of Walker and Hebets for raising millions of dollars for the Muhammand Ali Parkinson Research Center and Childhelp USA. Your support is making a difference in the lives of thousands of abused children.

Jimmy and Nancy Walker, Event Co-chairs
of Celebrity Fight Night in Phoenix, Arizona.

National Board of Directors

Founder/Chairman/CEO   Mrs. Sara O'Meara
Founder/President   Mrs. Yvonne Fedderson
Executive Vice President   Mr. Jim Hebets
Secretary-Treasurer   Miss Vita Cortese
Chaplain   Ms. Gloria Sutherland

Vice Presidents

The Honorable Nancy Brown
Mrs. Patti Edwards
Mr. Mark Feldman
Mrs. Marilyn McDaniel
Mr. Phil Odeen
Mrs. Connie Olsen
Mrs. Linda Willey
Mr. Armstrong Williams
Mr. Earl Worsham
Mr. Don Zimmer

Honorary Members

Mrs. Dolores Duncan
Mrs. Georgette Mosbacher
Mrs. Ann Vivian
Mrs. Julie Wrigley

Childhelp USA—National Advisory Board

General and Mrs. James Abrahamson
The Honorable Thomas J. Bliley
The Honorable Bill Bradley
Mrs. Barbara Bush
The Honorable Ben Nighthorse Campbell
Mrs. Rosalyn Carter
The Honorable Dan Coats
The Honorable and Mrs. Christopher Cox
The Honorable Bud Cramer
The Honorable John C. Danforth
The Honorable Dennis DeConcini
Father Ralph DiOrio
The Honorable and Mrs. Christopher Dodd
The Honorable Elizabeth Dole
The Honorable David Dreier
Dr. Vincent J. Fontana
Mrs. Jane Gephardt
Rev. Billy Graham
The Honorable James M. Inhofe
The Honorable Jack Kemp
C. Everett Koop, M.D.
The Honorable and Mrs. Jon Kyl
The Honorable and Mrs. Trent Lott
General Robert F. McDermott
The Honorable Barbara Mikulski
Admiral William Owens
The Honorable Harry Pregerson
Mrs. Nancy Reagan
The Honorable Charles Robb
The Honorable Matt Salmon
The Honorable Paul Sarbanes
Mr. Willard Scott
Robert Sigholtz, Ph.D.

Mr. Allen E. Susman
The Honorable John Warner
The Honorable and Mrs. Pete Wilson
The Honorable Frank Wolf
Mr. Randolph C. Wood
Mr. Efrem Zimbalist, Jr.

Childhelp USA Chapters and Auxiliaries

Arizona
> Greater Phoenix
> Greater Sedona

California
> Buena Ventura—Los Angeles and Thousand Oaks
> Angels (Music and Entertainment Industry)—
> > Los Angeles and Thousand Oaks
> Eagles—Los Angeles and Thousand Oaks
> Wheel Friends (Custom Wheel Industry)—
> > Los Angeles and Thousand Oaks
> Inland Empire—San Bernardino County
> Greater Los Angeles
> Orange County
> Riverside
> Greater San Diego

District of Columbia
> Washington Area

Michigan
> Greater Detroit
> Grand Rapids

Tennessee
> Nashville
> Knoxville

Virginia
    Lake of the Woods—Locust Grove
    South Hampton Roads—Virginia Beach

Foundations

Over the years we have been blessed to receive generous financial support from *many* wonderful foundations. While we deeply appreciate each foundation for its much-needed assistance, space constraints allow us to acknowledge only a handful whose constancy and dedication to our work has helped Childhelp USA become what it is today.

Angels Care
Arizona Foundation For Women
Celebrity Fight Night Foundation, Inc.
Cendant Charitable Foundation
The Cody Foundation
Nathan Cummings Foundation, Inc.
Walt Disney Foundation
Rhonda Fleming Foundation
Geddes Philanthropic Trust
The Gerber Foundation and Gerber Products
Bruce T. Halle Family Foundation
Conrad N. Hilton Foundation
In-N-Out Burger Foundation
Justice for Athletes
Thomas and Dorothy Leavey Foundation
Alex and Marie Manoogian Foundation
Richard and Jane Manoogian Foundation
P.K. Foundation
Variety—The Children's Charity of Southern California
Weingart Foundation
Julie Ann Wrigley Foundation

Childhelp USA Programs and Services

Childhelp USA National Child Abuse Hotline
1-800-4-A-CHILD (1-800-422-4453)

Residential Treatment Facilities (Villages)

Children's Advocacy Centers

Mobile Advocacy Centers

Child Abuse Prevention, Education, and Training Programs

Foster Care

Group Homes

Special Friends

Circle of Angels

Eagles

State Boards

Chapter Volunteers

Wheel Friends

For additional information, or a list of our volunteer chapters throughout the United States and opportunities to participate, please visit our Website at www.childhelpusa.org.

Appeal

Ninety-one cents of every dollar spent goes directly to Childhelp USA programs benefiting children. If you are interested in making a difference in the life of an abused child by financially supporting Childhelp USA, you may send your contribution to:

Childhelp USA
15757 N. 78th St.
Scottsdale, Arizona 85260
(480) 922-8212
(480) 922-7061 (fax)
www.childhelpusa.org

Childhelp Inc., doing business as Childhelp USA®, was incorporated April 21, 1960 and is a 501(c)(3) tax-exempt public charity. Donations and gifts are tax-deductible as allowed by law. Childhelp Inc.'s Federal Taxpayer I.D. Number is 95-2884608.

We hope this Jodere Group book has benefited you in your quest for personal, intellectual, and spiritual growth.

Jodere Group is passionate about bringing new and exciting books, such as *Silence Broken*, to readers worldwide. Our company was created as a unique publishing and multimedia avenue for individuals whose mission it is to impact the lives of others positively. We recognize the strength of an original thought, a kind word, and a selfless act—and the power of the individuals who possess them. We are committed to providing the support, passion, and creativity necessary for these individuals to achieve their goals and dreams.

Jodere Group is comprised of a dedicated and creative group of people who strive to provide the highest quality of books, audio programs, online services, and live events to people who pursue life-long learning. It is our personal and professional commitment to embrace our authors, speakers, and readers with helpfulness, respect, and enthusiasm.

For more information about our products, authors, or live events, please call (800) 569-1002 or visit us on the Web at **www.jodere.com.**

JODERE
GROUP